NO-SEW
SOFT FURNISHINGS

NO-SEW
SOFT FURNISHINGS

QUICK AND EASY TECHNIQUES FOR EFFECTIVE HOME FURNISHINGS

JULIET BAWDEN
PHOTOGRAPHS BY SHONA WOOD

WARD LOCK

A WARD LOCK BOOK

First published in the UK 1998
by Ward Lock
Wellington House
125 Strand
LONDON
WC2R 0BB
www. cassell.co.uk

A Cassell Imprint

Created and produced by
Rosemary Wilkinson Publishing
38 Halton Road, London N1 2EU

Copyright © Juliet Bawden and
Rosemary Wilkinson 1998

NOTE
Imperial and metric
measurements are not
direct conversions. Follow
only one set of measurements
in each project.

Distributed in the United States by
Sterling Publishing Co., Inc.
387 Park Avenue South, New York,
NY 10016-8810

A British Library Cataloguing in
Publication Data block for this book may
be obtained from the British Library

Designed by Mason Linklater
Edited by Rosemary Wilkinson
Template illustrations by Stephen Dew

ISBN 0 7063 7770 2

Printed by
Midas Printing, Hong Kong

Contents

Introduction

IN THIS BOOK I HAVE SHOWN HOW TO USE THE LATEST MATERIALS AND EQUIPMENT TO REPLACE THE SEWING MACHINE AND ACHIEVE PRACTICAL, STYLISH AND CONTEMPORARY FURNISHINGS AT SPEED FOR THE HOME. I HAVE CHOSEN PROJECTS TO MAKE THE BEST USE OF THE DIFFERENT PRODUCTS AVAILABLE. NO-SEW HEADING TAPE, FOR EXAMPLE, IS PERFECT FOR UNLINED CURTAINS, INEXPENSIVE MUSLIN CAN BE HEMMED INSTANTLY WITH FUSIBLE BONDING WEB AND MADE INTO CAFÉ CURTAINS, SWAGS AND BED DRAPES, EYELET KITS CAN BE USED CREATIVELY TO PRODUCE CUSHIONS, FUTON COVERS AND BLINDS.

AS WELL AS THESE EXCITING NEW SOFT FURNISHING PROJECTS, THERE ARE ALSO IDEAS FOR RENOVATING EXISTING FURNITURE. YOU CAN TRANSFORM A PLAIN TOY BOX USING PAINTED CANVAS, APPLIQUÉED MOTIFS AND A GLUE GUN, ADD CURTAINS TO A WARDROBE OR A SET OF BOOK SHELVES AND RE-COVER AN OLD-FASHIONED SCREEN. AND THERE ARE IDEAS FOR USING RUGS, SHAWLS AND PURCHASED SHEETS CREATIVELY TO MAKE INSTANT AND EFFECTIVE HOME FURNISHINGS.

SOME OF THE PRODUCTS USED IN THE BOOK COME IN KIT FORM, OTHERS JUST AS USEFUL TOOLS. THERE ARE INNOVATIONS, SUCH AS CAFÉ CLIPS WHICH WILL TRANSFORM A PLAIN PIECE OF FABRIC, A BLANKET OR BEDSPREAD INTO A CURTAIN. BUTTON KITS, FOR COVERING WITH A CHOSEN FABRIC, NOW COME WITH A PIN ON THE BACK AND A BUTTERFLY CLIP TO KEEP THEM IN PLACE. NO-SEW LAMPSHADE AND TIEBACK KITS COME WITH EVERYTHING YOU

NEED TO MAKE INDIVIDUAL ACCESSORIES, YOU JUST PROVIDE THE FABRIC TO MATCH YOUR OWN COLOUR SCHEME.

H ERE ARE OVER SIXTY IDEAS FOR BREAKFAST ROOMS, LIVING ROOMS, BEDROOMS, CHILDREN'S ROOMS AND EVEN THE HOME OFFICE, SO THAT YOU CAN REJUVENATE YOUR HOME WITHOUT EVER SEWING A STITCH. IT HAS BEEN GREAT FUN MAKING EVERYTHING FOR THIS BOOK AND I HOPE THAT THE MANY PHOTOGRAPHS AND CLEAR INSTRUCTIONS WILL INSPIRE YOU TO TRY OUT THE IDEAS FOR YOUR OWN HOMES.

JULIET BAWDEN

INTRODUCTION

Tools and Materials

In order to make truly "no-sew" fabric furnishings, without the aid of needle, thread or sewing machine, there have to be excellent substitutes. These take the form of handy small tools and a purpose-made range of materials which aid with the hanging, hemming and bonding of fabrics.

The ease with which these projects can be made mean that you can change your room style frequently but some of the methods have their limitations: the ribbon tie and eyelet blinds, for example, are best used for blinds that will be left in one position most of the time; tab-top curtains will not stand up to vigorous opening and closing. Other methods are perfect solutions to personalising your interior decorations: no-sew lampshades enable you to co-ordinate the furnishings closely and stapled bedhead covers produce lasting features in an individually designed bedroom. The following list describes the range of tools and materials used throughout this book.

Glue gun and glue sticks; fusible hemming tape, with and without paper backing; fusible webbing; popper tape; scissors and tape measure.

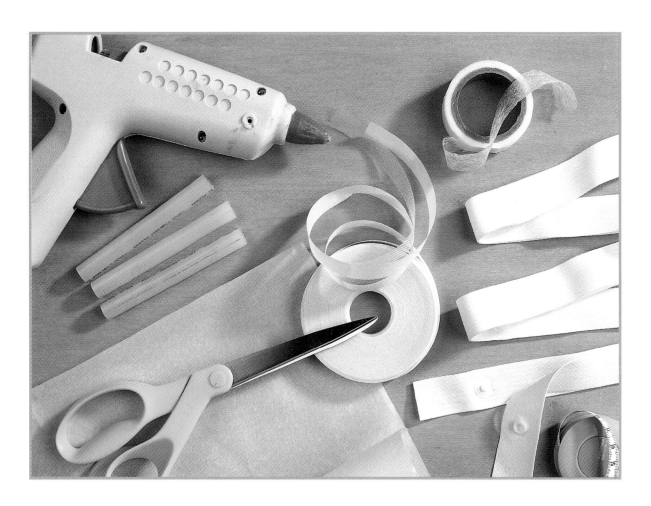

TOOLS & MATERIALS

TOOLS

Glue Gun

A glue gun is a dispenser of glue in the shape of a pistol. It heats up a glue stick which is pushed into the rear of the gun and dispenses liquid glue to all manner of objects. When the gun has heated up, pull the trigger and you can push the glue through the nozzle in a thin strip to cover large areas, in small spots to tackle the tiniest nooks and crannies and even in specific patterns, if necessary.

The drying time for such glues is generally quite quick, usually within seconds. There are two sorts of glue gun: hot melt and cool melt.

Cool melt glue guns are designed with safety in mind with features, including a light, bracket, rubber-covered nozzle and ready-attached plug. There is a five minute heating time to soften the glue and when the glue comes out it is easily controlled with the sensitive trigger. It is quite stringy, but because it cools quickly the strings can be removed almost immediately.

A glue gun is used most often for projects which need a very firm bond, especially when to use a fusible webbing, which needs to be damp to work, is inappropriate, for example, on canvas which usually shrinks when wet. It is used for bonding heavyweight fabrics and for attaching loosely woven trimmings.

Staple Gun

This excellent tool is a must when attaching fabric or Velcro to hard surfaces. Staple guns come in different weights and use different sized staples. Choose the most robust staple gun you can afford and buy plenty of staples, as it is infuriating to run out in the middle of a job.

Iron and Ironing Board

Buy the best domestic iron you can afford. It should be as heavy as possible for pressing and should be a steam iron, as the fusible webbing used in this book needs steam to enable the glue to work. You will need a large ironing board for pressing large areas of fabric.

Scissors

Dressmaking scissors with 20-22cm (8-9in) blades are needed for cutting large areas of fabric. You will also need small embroidery-type scissors for snipping off ends and paper scissors for pattern cutting. Always keep paper and fabric scissors separate. Paper will blunt scissors. It is worth investing in a scissors sharpener. Pinking shears are good if you wish to stop fabric fraying or to make a decorative edge.

MATERIALS

Fusible Hemming Tape

These tapes are the solution to making hems without sewing. They are available in two versions, one with a paper backing, under the brand name of Bondahem, and one without, known as Wundaweb. Using the paper-backed version is a two-stage process. The tape and paper carrier are ironed onto the first surface, then the paper is peeled off and the second surface pressed in position before being ironed to bond. Always place a damp cloth over the tape before ironing in position, to increase the bonding property.

Fusible Webbing

Fusible webbing (brand name Bondaweb) is sold by the metre and is used to bond one fabric to another. It is particularly useful for appliqué work. It comes with a paper backing on which the appliqué design can be drawn, then cut out. The webbing is placed, paper side up, on the appliqué fabric, then bonded with a hot iron. The design is cut out of the fabric, then the paper backing is peeled off and the fabric and webbing placed, webbing side down, on the backing fabric. A damp cloth is placed on top and the fabric sandwich is ironed to bond. Test to see if the two fabrics have bonded by trying to lift a corner. If not, repeat the ironing.

No-Sew Heading Tape

Heading tape for curtains is now available in no-sew versions and in a variety of styles. We have used the pencil pleat and the standard versions for curtains in this book. The tapes have lines of glue which are bonded to the curtain fabric using a hot iron.

Hook and Loop Tape
Hook and loop tape is usually known by the brand name, Velcro. It comes in many widths, in spot form and in different colours. It is very strong and allows surfaces to be joined together and pulled apart. It comes in a sticky-backed and a non-sticky backed version. There is also a type which has one sticky side and one non-sticky. The sticky side can be stuck to hard surfaces, the non-sticky side will need to be applied using a glue gun or fabric glue.

Popper Tape
Poppers are available in tape form which are perfect for fastening duvet covers or, as in our Dining Chair Cover, for closing the back of the covering. The strips are glued into position.

Café Clips and Swag Finials
There are two main types of café clip. The first has a loop at the top which hooks onto a curtain ring and a clip at the bottom, which holds fabric between its jaws like a clothes peg.

The second type is an integrated ring and clip. Often the clip part is serrated to help grip the fabric better. When using clips like these, it is necessary to support the weight of the curtain until it is evenly hung, otherwise the weight of the fabric will pull it out of the jaws of the clips.

Finials hold fabric for swags in position both firmly and decoratively.

Eyelet Kit
Eyelet kits come with the eyelet which is made in two parts, a device which both punches a hole for the eyelet and holds one half of the eyelet in position while it is being inserted and another part for placing under the fabric and holding the other half in position. You need to work on a firm surface. If the fabric is thick, you will find it easier to cut a hole with a craft knife, rather than using the punch provided. Make sure that you choose the correct size of piping cord to fit the diameter of the eyelet.

FABRICS

Medium and Lightweight Fabrics
When choosing fabrics for soft furnishings, whether sewn or not, first consider the use to which they will be put. A fabric for a kitchen chair cover will need to be hardwearing and machine washable. Fabrics for throws and sofa coverings need to be fluid and comfortable, they should drape well and yet be warm against the skin. For no-sew soft furnishings, medium and lightweight fabrics are generally better than heavy

Hook and loop tape; no-sew heading tape; eyelet kit and piping cord; staple gun and staples; a selection of café clips and finials.

10

weight. Use wide furnishing fabrics for bedcovers, throws and tablecloths, so that you do not have to join two widths.

Sheer Fabrics

These make perfect curtains for windows where you wish to hide the view but still want the light to come through. They hang beautifully and make marvellous drapes for a four-poster bed.

Linens

We have used natural linen for the tablecloth and napkins. Linen is expensive but very hardwearing and stands up well to repeated washing.

Canvas

Canvas comes in wide widths which makes it suitable for floor cloths or blinds for wide windows. It should be washed before use, as it shrinks and distorts. It is also a heavyweight fabric and will need to be glued rather than bonded with fusible hemming tape.

Non-fraying Fabric

Funtex is the trade name for a non-fraying fabric which has been manufactured with the craft market in mind. It comes in a variety of bright colours and is machine washable, which makes it more suitable than felt for soft furnishings. If used for appliqué, as in the children's Room Tidy on page 118, it is best used with fusible webbing, as glue tends to show through the surface.

DYES

There are various different types of dyes available depending on the quantity of fabric you are dyeing, the method you are using and the type of fabric being dyed.

Multi-purpose dyes are ideal for dyeing small pieces of cloth by hand and may also be used in a washing machine for larger pieces. They are suitable for use with natural fabrics, nylon and

A selection of dyes suitable for dyeing small and large pieces of fabric, by hand and machine.

garments containing Lycra.

Hand dyes are perfect for dyeing smaller items. They are designed for use with hot tap water and are suitable for cotton, linen, and viscose.

Cold water dyes are ideal for special effects, such as batik, tie dye and grade dyeing. They are suitable for dyeing natural fabrics by hand.

Grade Dyeing

The variable colouring of the muslin for the Four Poster Tiebacks on page 104 was achieved by grade dyeing. This very effective dyeing method is carried out by wrapping parts of the cloth in plastic to protect it whilst dyeing other parts. To make the muslin for the tieback, three colours were used: red, pink and orange. First dye the muslin completely in pink, then wrap one third up in cling film and dye the rest in orange. Finally wrap half the remainder of the fabric in cling film and dye the rest in red.

LIVING
ROOMS

THIS IS THE ROOM FOR RELAXING IN AND
ENTERTAINING FRIENDS, SO IT NEEDS TO BE
BOTH STYLISH AND COMFORTABLE. CHANGING THE
SOFT FURNISHINGS IS A GOOD WAY OF GIVING THE
ROOM A NEW LOOK WITHOUT MAJOR EXPENSE; WITH
NO-SEW TECHNIQUES, THIS CAN BE DONE QUICKLY
AND SIMPLY. WE HAVE CREATED FULL-LENGTH
CURTAINS USING TAB-TOPS, AND SHOWN OTHER
INNOVATIVE IDEAS FOR WINDOWS. THERE ARE TWO
THROWS MADE IN THE SAME WAY BUT LOOKING
COMPLETELY DIFFERENT THROUGH THE CHOICE OF
FABRIC. CUSHIONS ARE AN EXCELLENT NO-SEW
PROJECT, ESPECIALLY IF YOU ARE NEW TO THE
TECHNIQUES. THE BASIC METHOD IS FOLLOWED BY
A VARIETY OF STYLES, SHAPES AND SIZES.

Simple Unlined Curtain

ADDING TABS INSTEAD OF CURTAIN HEADING TAPE IS A SIMPLE BUT ELEGANT WAY OF HANGING A CURTAIN. THE TABS ARE THREADED ONTO A POLE WHICH IN ITSELF BECOMES A FEATURE OF THE ROOM DECORATION. MANY ATTRACTIVE FINIALS FOR WOODEN AND METAL POLES ARE NOW AVAILABLE. THIS IS THE EASIEST KIND OF CURTAIN: UNLINED AND WITHOUT ANY SURFACE DECORATION, WHICH WILL SHOW AN ATTRACTIVE FABRIC TO BEST ADVANTAGE.

You will need

fabric (the width times the drop of the curtain plus 50cm (20in) for seam allowance plus enough fabric to make the tab headings – these are 30cm (12in) deep and 10cm (4in) wide. The number needed depends on the width of the window)

dressmaking scissors

Bondahem and iron

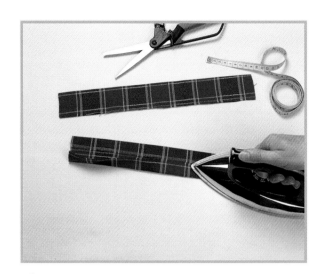

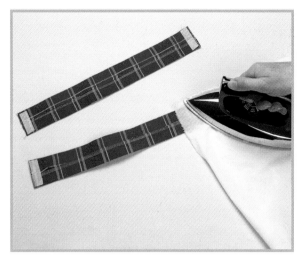

1 For the tabs, measure from the top of the curtain pole to the top of the window, double this measurement and add 5cm (2in). This gives the depth, the width is 10cm (4in). Work out the number of tabs required – ours are spaced every 11cm (4 ¼in) – and cut out. Fold each tab in half lengthwise and iron to mark the centre. Open out, then fold in each side to the marked centre line. Iron in place.

2 Cut two pieces of Bondahem the width of the tab and iron onto the wrong side of the tabs at the top and bottom short edges.

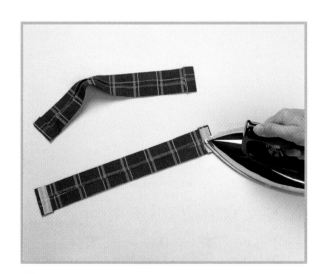

3 Remove the paper from the Bondahem and turn down the tops of the tabs. Cover with a damp cloth and iron to fuse the Bondahem. Repeat at the bottom of the tabs. Add another strip of Bondahem on top of the fold, iron and remove paper backing.

4 Cut two more pieces of Bondahem as before. Measure 5cm (2in) down from each end of the tabs and iron on the strips. Remove the paper backing. These extra pieces will help the adhesion of the tabs to the curtain top.

5 Iron Bondahem along the top edge of the wrong side of the curtain. Remove the backing paper, fold over the fabric and cover with a damp cloth. Iron to bond. For the sides and hem, iron a narrow hem, then iron Bondahem over the fold and continue as before.

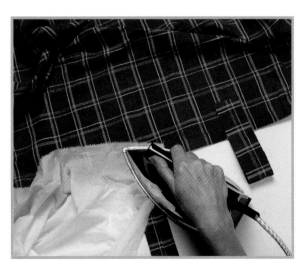

6 Place the tab flat in position at the top of the curtain, so that the inner strip of Bondahem aligns with the curtain edge. Cover with a damp cloth and iron in position. Fold over the tab and iron in place to the reverse of the curtain in the same way. Thread the pole through the tabs and hang the curtain.

▲ SHEER DECORATION

Use this simple treatment for a window for which you do not need a drawn curtain. I have used a sheer, self-patterned muslin. Add Bondahem to the top and bottom as described opposite, then simply wrap the fabric loosely around the pole. Tuck one end into the folds and leave the rest of the curtain hanging to one side of the window.

▶ A RUG CURTAIN

This is the simplest of all curtains but nonetheless effective. Choose a lightweight rug which will fit the dimensions of your window. Turn over a small heading at the top and attach café clips evenly spaced along the fold. Add curtain rings to the clips and thread onto a pole.

Padded Tiebacks

THERE ARE SOME VERY GOOD KITS FOR TIEBACKS, WHICH SUPPLY EVERYTHING EXCEPT THE FABRIC AND IT IS ONE OF THESE WHICH WE HAVE CHOSEN HERE AND WE GIVE THREE ALTERNATIVES WITHOUT A KIT, SHOWN ON PAGE 23.

You will need

kit, including pattern, iron-on interfacing, wadding, hemming webbing and D rings

dressmaking scissors

fabric

iron

glue gun and glue sticks

trim – the length of curved edge of tieback plus turnings

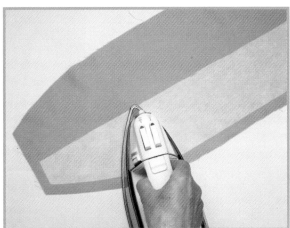

1 Using the pattern provided in the kit as a guide, cut out the fabric. Place right side down on the work surface and position the interfacing over one half, leaving a 1.5cm (½in) allowance at the sides and bottom. Iron in place.

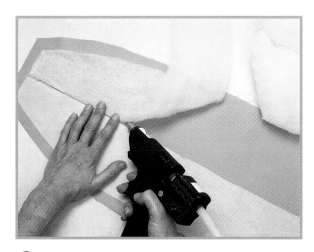

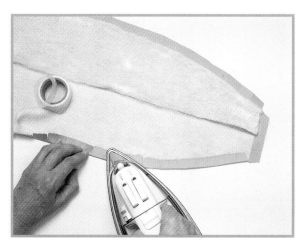

2 Place the wadding over the other half of the fabric, aligning the long edges. Using the glue gun, fix the wadding to the fabric at one or two points along the edges.

3 Cut notches in the seam at regular intervals and trim the excess fabric at the corners. Place hemming webbing all round the edge of the interfacing and wadding. Fold the notched seam over onto the webbing and iron in place.

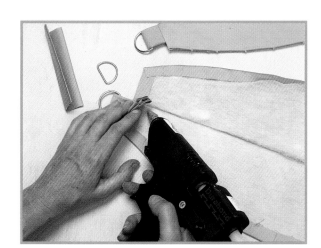

4 Prepare loops by cutting two pieces of fabric 12 x 10cm (4 ¾ x 4in). Fold and glue both long edges to the centre. Fold in half lengthwise and glue again. Slide the tabs through a D ring and fold in half crosswise. Place the D ring tab at the end of the tieback, so that one edge aligns with the centre of the tieback. Glue in place. Fold the tieback in half along the centre line and use hemming webbing to secure.

5 Using a glue gun, attach the bobble trim onto the lower outside edge of the tieback.

◀ **TWISTED ROPE TIEBACK**
Make a long tieback for a floor length, unlined curtain using three lengths of furnishing cord as described on page 23.

Simple Swag

S WAGS ARE ONE OF THOSE SOFT FURNISHING FLOURISHES WHICH SEEM TO GO IN AND OUT OF FASHION. THE ONE WE HAVE MADE HERE IS MADE FROM A CONTEMPORARY SHEER FABRIC AND IS TWISTED ROUND TWO PURCHASED FINIALS. THE HANGING IS SIMPLICITY ITSELF, SO ONCE THE HOLDERS ARE IN PLACE, THE SWAG CAN BE CHANGED AS OFTEN AS YOU LIKE, PERHAPS TO MAKE A SUMMER AND WINTER WINDOW TREATMENT.

You will need

2.5m (2 ³/4yds) organza or other easily draped fabric

Bondahem and iron

2 swag finials

L I V I N G   R O O M S

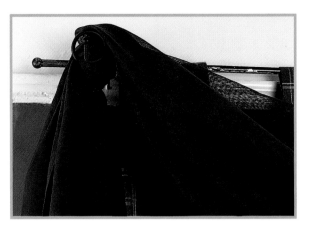

1 Fold over a 1cm (³⁄₈in) hem on each short edge of the fabric. Place Bondahem on the turnover and iron in place over a damp cloth. Remove the paper backing, fold the hem over again and iron in place as before.

2 Attach the swag finials to the wall above and at either side of the curtain rail. Drape the fabric so that it hangs centrally over both finials. Arrange the central part so that it hangs in neat folds, then twist the fabric loosely through the curly parts of the finials.

◄ LIGHT AND DARK

Use a lightweight fabric for this type of swag, especially if the colour is dark. Organza is a perfect choice.

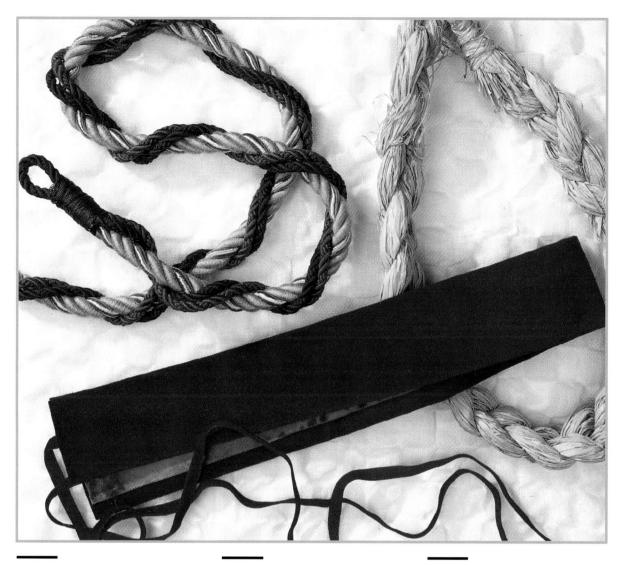

TWISTED ROPE TIEBACK

To make the tieback shown in the photograph on page 20, use a tape measure to judge how much rope is needed. Loop it round the curtain in the place it will hang, note the measurement, then add 15cm (6in) for the loops. You will need three ropes to this length. Twist two thin, contrast-coloured ropes round one thicker one and make a loop at each end with one of the thin ropes. Trim the excess rope. Secure the loop and cut ends by winding embroidery cotton tightly round the ropes.

RED VELVET TIEBACK

To make the tieback shown in the photograph on page 14, use a tape measure as described left, then add 3cm (1$\frac{1}{4}$in) for turnings. Cut a piece of red velvet to this measurement and 13cm (5in) wide. Turn in the two long edges to the centre and use iron-on webbing to secure in place. Hem the short edges in the same way. Glue one end of a length of narrow ribbon in the centre of each end of the tieback, then glue a wide piece of ribbon over the back to cover the raw edges.

RAFFIA TIEBACK

Plaited raffia makes an unusual tieback suitable for heavy curtain fabric, such as the rug curtain on page 17. To make the tieback, make a normal three-strand plait, then loop each end and bind with raffia to hold in place.

Twisted Silk Lampshade

THIS SOPHISTICATED LAMPSHADE IS VERY SIMPLE TO MAKE. THE SECRET IS NOT TO USE TOO MUCH FABRIC, SO THAT THE LIGHT WILL SHINE THROUGH. THE STIFFENER USED ON THE FABRIC ALSO ACTS AS AN ADHESIVE, SO THAT STRIPS CAN BE EASILY JOINED. TO FIREPROOF THE SHADE, USE A FIRE RETARDANT FROM A THEATRICAL SUPPLIERS.

You will need

about 1m (1yd) silk fabric
dressmaking scissors
fabric stiffener as used for making window blinds
container and brush for the fabric stiffener
a plain lampshade – paper or fabric is suitable

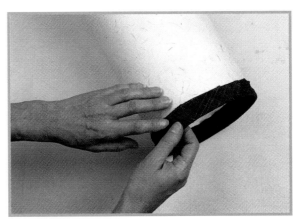

1 Find the diagonal line of the fabric by laying the fabric flat on a work surface and bringing the bottom lefthand corner up to the top edge. Cut strips of fabric parallel to the fold, 8cm (3¼in) wide. The number of strips you will need depends on the size of the lamp and the density of the fabric.

2 Cut one narrow diagonal strip, about 4cm (1½in) wide. Mix the stiffener according to the manufacturer's instructions. This is usually about one part stiffener to four parts water. Brush the stiffener onto the narrow strip so it is soaked through. Place the fabric over the rim of the lamp. Overlap the ends, folding over the top edge to neaten.

3 Brush stiffener onto one of the wider pieces, so that it is thoroughly wet. Leave to one side as you do the next piece. Do not be concerned about the milky appearance, this will disappear when the fabric dries.

4 Take one of the wet pieces, tuck one end just inside the shade and wrap round the shade in a shallow spiral, scrunching it up slightly as you do so. To join a new piece, place over the top of the previous one, overlapping the edges slightly and tucking raw edges out of sight. The stiffener will help it stick to the previous strip and to the shade. At the bottom of the lamp, trim the edge at an angle and fold the end up to the inside of the lamp. Leave to dry overnight.

26

◄ **PURPLE LAMPSHADE**

Another example of the lampshade
technique described and illustrated
on page 24. This is a quick and
economical way of making a
lampshade to coordinate with the
rest of your room decoration,
perhaps matching the curtain
fabric or using the shade as an
accent colour, which could also be
picked up in the cushions.

▶ RED SILK LAMPSHADE

The technique for stiffening fabric strips and twisting them onto an existing plain shade can be used for all kinds of lamps. It works well on a standard lamp for example. Try to keep the fabric strips evenly spaced, as the overlaps will be accentuated when the light is turned on.

Ribbon Tied Blind

A S AN ALTERNATIVE TO A VENETIAN OR ROLLER BLIND FOR A GLAZED DOOR OR A WINDOW, USE A PIECE OF MEDIUM WEIGHT FABRIC AND TIE IT IN POSITION WITH RIBBON TIES. THIS TREATMENT IS ONLY SUITABLE FOR WINDOWS WHERE YOU WILL NOT BE REGULARLY RAISING AND LOWERING THE BLIND.

You will need

Bondahem and iron
fabric to cover the width of the window plus 3cm
(1¼in) and the length from the top of the window to
the floor plus 6cm (2½in)
ribbon 4 times the length of the fabric
stick-on Velcro – the length of width of blind
glue gun and glue sticks

1 Place Bondahem along one of the side edges of the fabric on the wrong side. Iron in place over a damp cloth. Remove the paper backing, fold over the fabric to cover the Bondahem and iron in place as before. Repeat on the other side.

2 Fold over 1.5cm (½in) at the top of the fabric. Iron Bondahem on top of the fold over a damp cloth. Remove the paper backing, fold the fabric over again and iron in place as before. Repeat at the bottom of the fabric.

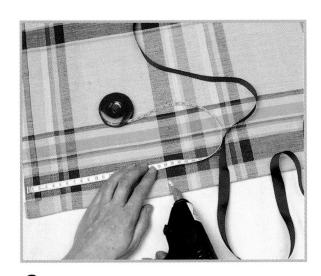

3 Cut the ribbon into two equal pieces and fold each piece in half to mark the centre. Measure 20cm (8in) in from each side of the blind at the top and glue each piece of ribbon at its central point to the top of the fabric, so that it hangs vertically.

4 Glue the non sticky side of the Velcro along the top edge of the blind, so that half the ribbon is on the wrong side and the other half on the right side. Press the other side of the Velcro to the wooden part of the window frame. Fix the blind in position by pressing the Velcro strips together. Roll up the bottom of the blind neatly and hold in position by tying the ribbons into bows.

velope Cushion

CUSHIONS ARE THE FINISHING TOUCHES TO A ROOM. THEY NOT ONLY ADD SOFTNESS AND COMFORT, THEY CAN ALSO BE USED TO PULL TOGETHER AN UNCOORDINATED COLOUR SCHEME. THE ENVELOPE OVERLAP AT THE BACK OF THIS CUSHION DOES AWAY WITH THE NEED FOR ZIPS OR OTHER CLOSINGS, MAKING THIS A VERY SIMPLE COVER WHICH CAN BE EASILY REMOVED FOR WASHING.

You will need

fabric to cover the front and back of the pad plus ⅓ of the height of the back of the cushion pad

dressmaking scissors

square cushion pad

Bondahem and iron

fusible hemming tape

Variation

A circular cushion could be made in the same way. Try glueing or bonding a trimming round the edges of the finished cushion.

1 Cut one square of fabric the size of the cushion pad for the front and two pieces two-thirds the size of pad for the back, matching any pattern.

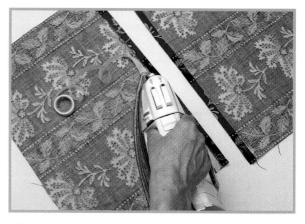

2 Fold over a 1cm (⅜in) hem on each of the long sides which will overlap on the two smaller pieces. Iron Bondahem on top, remove the paper backing, fold over the hem and iron in place again.

LIVING ROOMS

3 With right sides together, use fusible hemming tape to bond one back piece to the front piece at the sides and bottom, so that the hemmed side is in the centre of the cushion back.

4 Place the second back piece on top aligning raw edges and with the hemmed side in the centre. Bond to the front and back pieces along the sides and top. Trim the seams and excess fabric at the corners. Turn to the right side and insert the cushion pad.

PATCHWORK BOLSTER

To fit a bolster with a circumference of 57cm (22½in) and 51cm (20in) long, you will need five pieces of assorted fabrics each measuring 13.5 x 60cm (6 x 23½in), four pieces of ribbon 60cm (23½in) long, two pieces of ribbon, 50cm (18in) long, Bondahem and an iron. Using Bondahem, fuse the five pieces together down their long sides to make a long strip. Bond the four strips of ribbon over the seams, then neaten the two short ends. Fold the fabric in half, right sides together and Bondahem the seam. Turn the tube to the right side, insert the bolster pad centrally. Tie each end with ribbon.

ORGANZA COVERED CUSHION

Make a glamorous two-cover cushion to make the most of the glittering transparent quality of metallic organza. Make a fitting cushion cover from plain red or maroon silk, using the envelope method described on page 30. Make an outer cushion cover from red and orange organza shot with gold. Cut two pieces 5cm (2in) larger all round than the cushion pad. Turn under and bond a hem on one of the sides of each piece. Place the two pieces right sides together, matching the hemmed edges. Bond the remaining three sides and turn through to the right side. This outer cover can be a permanent addition to the cushion or just slipped over the inner cover for evening entertaining.

VELVET CUSHION WITH GOLD CORD

This cushion is made in much the same way as the futon cover on page 84. For a cushion measuring 36cm (14in), cut two squares of velvet each measuring 56cm (22in). Make a 1cm (⅜in) single hem all round each piece and iron in place using Bondahem. Add large eyelets in each corner 9cm (3½in) from the edge, then at regular intervals in between. Make sure that the eyelets are in exactly the same position on both pieces. Thread a single length of thick gold cord through the eyelets in both layers and fasten at the front with a decorative bow.

RED SILK PILLOW CASE CUSHION

Cut two pieces of fabric, one to the dimensions of the cushion pad plus seam allowances all round and one 6cm (2½in) longer on one short side. Fold a double hem along the right hand short edge of both pieces, then place right sides together, aligning the three raw edges. Use fusible hemming tape to bond the three sides together. Turn right side out, insert the cushion pad and fold the flap inside the cushion.

Dining Chair Cover

IF YOUR DINING ROOM IS AN EXTENSION OF YOUR LIVING AREA, MAKING LOOSE COVERS FOR YOUR DINING CHAIRS IS A PRACTICAL WAY OF INTEGRATING THE COLOUR SCHEME THROUGHOUT. IT IS IMPORTANT TO CHOOSE A WASHABLE FABRIC FOR DINING CHAIRS.

You will need

brown paper or newspaper
paper and dressmaking scissors
fabric (see method)
Bondahem and iron
glue gun and glue sticks
poppers on a strip – the length should be the same as
the height of the chair back

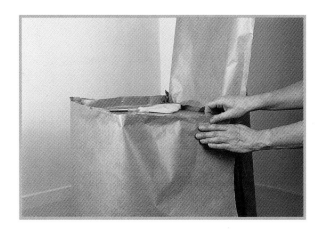

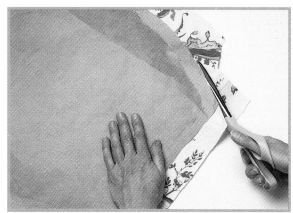

1 Place a piece of brown paper slightly larger than the chair seat on top of the seat and press it against the chair to mark the outline. Cut the paper, so that it has a border of 1cm (⅜in) all round larger than the chair seat. Repeat for the front of the chair back and the skirt. Note that the skirt will be one piece of fabric extending round three sides. Measure the back in two sections with an allowance for a seam down the centre back. Pin the pieces together on the chair and make any adjustments needed.

2 Unpin and remove the pattern pieces, then lay side by side to work out how much material is needed. Pin each pattern piece onto fabric and cut out. Pin the fabric pieces, wrong sides together, on the chair and check for fit. Adjust as necessary, then remove the cover from the chair.

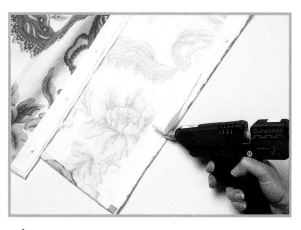

3 Use the Bondahem to attach the pieces, right sides together. It may be easier to glue gun curved sections. Before attaching the back pieces to the front, fold in the seam allowance of one centre edge and bond. Overlap this seam over the raw edge of the other back piece. Pin, then bond to the front.

4 Using the glue gun, fix the popper strip to either side of the centre seam at the back. Place the cover on the chair and press the popper strips together to close.

William Morris Throw

WHEN MAKING A THROW THERE ARE VARIOUS POINTS TO CONSIDER, SUCH AS THE WEIGHT OF THE FABRIC, THE WAY IT DRAPES, WILL IT BE PURELY DECORATIVE OR IS IT GOING TO BE NEEDED FOR WARMTH AND COMFORT? THIS THROW IS IN AN EASY-CARE COTTON, WHICH IS PRACTICAL AS WELL AS PRETTY.

◄ Choose a furnishing fabric, so that you do not need to join strips to make the required width. The main fabric is a square, the border strips are 10cm (4in) wide and 10cm (4in) longer than the sides of the centre square, giving a 3.5cm (1⅜in) double border. Follow the instructions for the Tablecloth on page 40.

Checked Silk Throw

I N COMPLETE CONTRAST, THIS THROW IS
FLAMBOYANT AND RICH, WITH TIGHTLY
WOVEN FURNISHING SILK AT ITS CENTRE
AND A MITRED BORDER OF HEAVYWEIGHT
SILK IN RASPBERRY PINK.

▲ To make it more of a feature, the border is wider
and measures 11cm (4$\frac{1}{2}$in) when finished. For this
you will need four strips 26cm (10 $\frac{1}{4}$in) wide and
26cm (10 $\frac{1}{4}$in) longer than the centre fabric.

L I V I N G   R O O M S

BREAKFAST ROOMS

THE DINING ROOM MAY BE ADJOINED TO THE KITCHEN OR IT MAY BE A SEPARATE ROOM. AS MANY OF US LIVE IN SMALL HOUSES AND APARTMENTS, WE OFTEN CHOOSE TO EAT IN THE SAME PLACE AS WE COOK, SO THE FURNISHINGS NEED TO BE PRACTICAL AS WELL AS DECORATIVE. IT IS IMPORTANT WHEN CHOOSING FABRICS FOR EATING AREAS THAT THEY WILL STAND UP TO REGULAR LAUNDERING. THE TYPE OF FABRIC AND DESIGN YOU CHOOSE WILL BE A REFLECTION OF YOUR OWN TASTES. HOWEVER, IF YOU CANNOT FIND A PATTERN YOU LIKE, IT IS EASY TO MAKE YOUR OWN DESIGNS BY DYEING, FREEHAND PAINTING OR STENCILLING ON PLAIN FABRIC. WE SHOW EXAMPLES OF THESE ALTERNATIVES.

Napkins and Tablecloth

THIS FRENCH PROVENÇAL FABRIC EVOKES ALL THAT IS BEST ABOUT KITCHENS AND BREAKFAST ROOMS. IT BRINGS TO MIND SUMMER HOLIDAYS AND RELAXED IDEAS OF SIMPLE LIVING WITH FRENCH BREAD AND COFFEE FOR BREAKFAST AND ALL DAY LONG TO LAZE AROUND READING THE PAPERS. CHOOSING THE SAME PATTERN IN TWO COLOURWAYS IS ALWAYS A SUCCESSFUL COMBINATION. THIS VERSATILE METHOD CAN ALSO BE USED TO MAKE BEDCOVERS AND THROWS.

You will need

a square of fabric for the centre of the tablecloth: the size will depend on the width of the fabric, ours was 127cm (50in)

contrast fabric to make the 4 border edges: the same width as the cloth plus 25cm (10in) and 100cm (40in) wide

fusible webbing and iron

glue gun and glue sticks

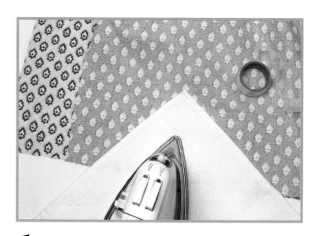

1 Cut out four strips from the contrast fabric, 25cm (10in) wide and 152cm (60in) long. Place the centre fabric over one of the border strips, right sides together, long edges aligned and with a 12.5cm (5in) overlap at each end. Using fusible hemming, bond the two pieces together along the edge.

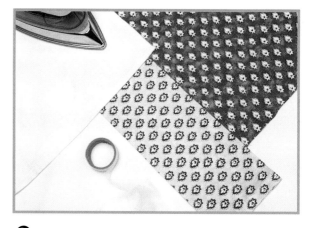

2 Fold over and press a 1.5cm (¾in) hem on the remaining long side of the border strip. Fold the strip over onto the centre fabric, so that it is folded exactly in half and bond to the wrong side of the centre fabric using fusible hemming. Repeat steps one and two on the opposite side. ▷ page 42

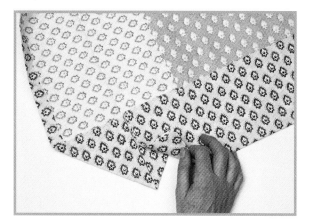

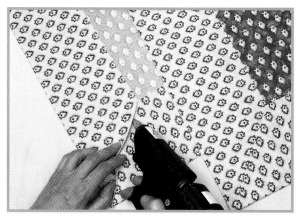

3 Repeat step one for the third side but stop the hemming tape 1.5cm (¾in) short of each corner. Fold over 1.5cm (¾in) on the remaining long side and iron in place, then fold over the same seam allowance on the two short sides. Fold the border strip exactly in half along its length and iron the crease. Open out, then at each corner bring the points over to the centre of the border strip to form the mitred corners. Bond the remaining border side to the wrong side of the centre fabric using fusible hemming, trimming the fabric so that it is enclosed by the mitre if necessary.

4 Using a glue gun, fix the diagonal fold at each mitred corner, front and back in place. Repeat steps three and four for the last border strip.

◄ **SIMPLE NAPKINS**
These napkins are quickly and simply made. Choose a fabric with a square pattern for maximum effect. You will need a 39cm (15in) square of fabric for each napkin. Turn over a double hem, 1 cm (⅜in) wide, on each side and use Bondahem, as described on page 16, step 5, to fuse in place.

Fringed Tablecloth and Napkins

THIS MUST BE THE EASIEST WAY TO MAKE A TABLECLOTH. IF YOU ARE LUCKY ENOUGH TO HAVE PURE LINEN, AS WE HAD, IT MAKES A VERY HARDWEARING CLOTH, OTHERWISE MADRAS COTTON IS ALSO A GOOD CHOICE.

▲ Dye the white linen for the tablecloth using a machine dye in bright yellow (see page 11). Iron while still damp with a steam iron. For the napkins, dye smaller pieces of fabric at least 42cm (16½in) square, using warm oranges and rusts. For small quantities of fabric, use multipurpose or cold water dyes (see page 11). Cut out and fringe the edges of the tablecloth and napkins as described opposite.

You will need

fabric 42cm (16 ½in) square for each napkin
fabric 210cm (83in) square for tablecloth
machine or multipurpose fabric dyes

1 For the napkins, measure a 40cm (16in) square keeping to the grain of the fabric. For the tablecloth, measure a 200cm (80in) square in the same way. Cut out carefully along the grain.

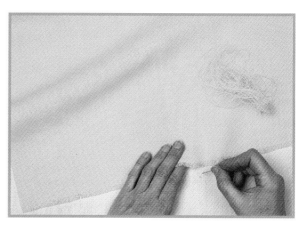

2 On each side, pull off any stray threads until you can pull whole threads away. Trim the uneven edges, then, using a pin, continue to pull away whole threads until you have a 1.5cm (½in) deep fringe on all four sides.

Café Curtain

You will need

fine fabric, such as a voile, which measures the height
of the finished curtain minus 5cm (2in) by one and a
half times the width of the window: we chose a
checked voile
Bondahem and iron
contrast fabric 25cm (10in) deep by one and a half
times the width of the window
curtain wire covered in plastic with an eye ring at each
end: the wire should be slightly shorter than the width
of the window, so that it is stretched to fit
2 cup hooks

Café curtains are usually curtains covering only the lower half of a window, so they give some privacy but you can still see out of the window. We have made a variety of café curtains to show just how different the same basic idea can look when made in a variety of different fabrics.

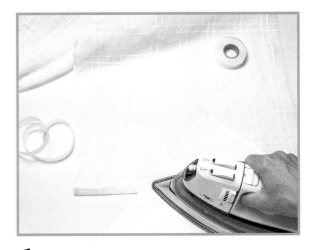

1 At each side of the checked voile, fold over and press 1.5cm (⅜in) to the wrong side. Iron Bondahem on top of the fold over a damp cloth. Remove the paper backing, fold over another 1.5cm (⅜in) and iron in place as before. Do the same with the sides of contrast fabric. ▷ *page 46*

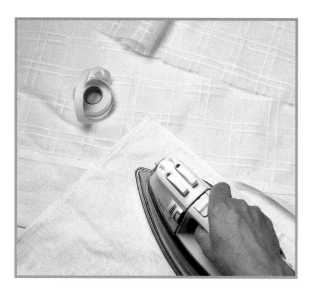

2 Place the checked voile and contrast fabric right sides together, aligning the two long raw edges and Bondahem together. Open out the two fabrics and iron the seam downwards. Fold and press a 1.5cm (³⁄₈in) hem along the remaining edge of the contrast fabric. Fold it down onto the wrong side of checked voile, matching the previous seam. Bondahem this edge in place.

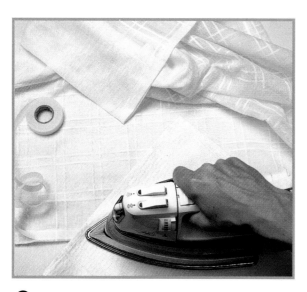

3 At the top of the curtain fold over 1.5cm (³⁄₈in) to the wrong side and press, then fold over another 3cm (1 ¼in). Bondahem along the folded edge to make a channel.

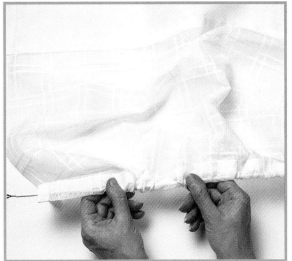

4 Thread the wire through the channel. Screw in cup hooks on either side of the window at the height required for the curtain and attach the curtain wire to the hooks.

◄ **BORDERED VOILE**

This café curtain is made with a plain voile border. Other fabrics could be used but keep to lightweights.

▲ PINK FLORAL CAFÉ CURTAIN

This fifties' inspired curtain fabric by designer Kath Kitson is just right for a pretty kitchen. Rather than using one and a half times the width of the window, take three times the width to make a very full curtain. This is a simpler version of the curtain on page 45, as it has no border. Simply hem the sides and bottom and make the channel as before, then glue pink rick-rack braid just above the bottom edge.

▶ STENCILLED CHILLI CURTAIN

Calico is an inexpensive but plain fabric. It can be decorated easily and effectively using fabric paints either freehand or stencilled. The chilli design used here was stencilled and is given as a template on page 123. Use one and a half times the width of the window for the fabric and make up in the same way as the pink floral curtain.

◄ **INDIAN TIE-DYE SHAWL**
As a super quick alternative to making a café curtain, use a shawl or sarong and just drape it over the wire. This Indian shawl is particularly pretty and is made of very fine cotton so that it lets in the light.

Eyelet Blind

ROMAN BLINDS ARE A POPULAR WAY OF DRESSING WINDOWS. AS IT IS DIFFICULT TO MAKE A COMPLETELY NO-SEW ROMAN BLIND, WE HAVE MADE A SIMPLER VERSION USING EYELETS AND PIPING CORD ON STENCILLED CANVAS.

You will need

canvas the width and height of the window plus 10cm (4in) all round
dressmaking scissors
glue gun and glue sticks
marking pencil
eyelet kit and hammer
tracing paper and pencil
clear stencil acetate and stencil knife
masking tape
stencil brush
fabric paints: yellow, orange and green
stick-on Velcro the width of the blind
piping cord the same width as the eyelet hole 4 times the depth of the blind
plus 80cm (32in)

Note: canvas shrinks up to 10% when wet, so it is advisable to wash it before
commencing work.

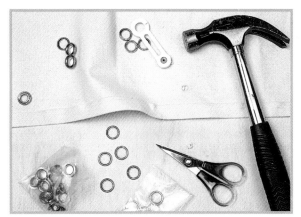

1 Measure the width and drop of the window, then add 10cm (4in) all round for shrinkage. Cut the canvas to size. Wash and dry the canvas, then check the size against the window, trimming to a 1cm (⅜in) seam allowance all round. Fold over the seam allowance, iron, then using a glue gun, stick the seams down.

2 Place the fabric against the window and mark the centre of each mullion or window pane with a marking pencil. Remove the fabric and make vertical rows of dots for the eyelets at the places marked and along the sides at intervals of 20cm (8in). Using the eyelet kit, insert eyelets at each marked point.

3 Trace off the design for the lemons and leaves from pages 122 and 123, transfer to clear acetate and cut out. Fix the stencils firmly to the right side of the canvas with masking tape and stencil a random design between the rows of eyelets. Hold the brush vertically and stipple on the paint so that it does not leak under the stencil. Paint the lemons in yellow and orange and the leaves in green. Leave to dry between each colour. Iron the cloth on the back to fix the design.

4 Place the sticky part of the Velcro above the window at the point where you will hang the blind. Using a glue gun attach the opposite part of the Velcro to the top edge of the blind on the wrong side. Cut the piping cord into four lengths, knot one end, then thread through each row of eyelets. Knot the bottom end close to the fabric and trim off the excess. Press the two pieces of Velcro together to hang the blind. To draw up the blind, push up the fabric and knot each cord.

Pelmet

A PELMET ADDS THE FINISHING TOUCH TO A WINDOW DRESSING. WE HAVE USED PELMFORM AS THE BASE, WHICH IS A DOUBLE-SIDED STICKY CARD SPECIFICALLY MADE FOR PELMETS AND TIEBACKS, IMPRINTED WITH VARIOUS EDGE PATTERNS. HOWEVER, WE HAVE CUT THE BACKING INTO A SIMPLE SHALLOW POINT TO MATCH THE INFORMAL KITCHEN WINDOW DRESSING.

You will need

Pelmform to the exact width of pelmet required
dressmaking scissors
a wooden batten the length of the pelmet
fabric the same size as the pelmet plus 3cm (1¼in) all round
backing fabric the same size as the pelmet
50cm (18in) pieces of orange and yellow felt fabric for decorating
Bondaweb and iron
glue gun and glue sticks
stick-on Velcro the length of the pelmet

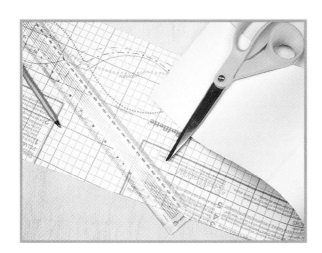

1 Measure the width of the window where the pelmet is to hang and decide on the depth at the sides and in the centre. Draw out the pattern on the Pelmform to the size measured, making a shallow V shape on the bottom edge, then cut out. Cut a batten the same width as the Pelmform and screw in place over the window.

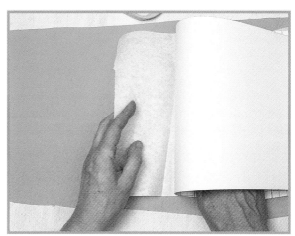

2 Place the fabric right side down on the work surface. Lift the backing paper in the centre of the Pelmform, cut it, then peel back a little on each side. Place the Pelmform centrally on top of the fabric, with the cut side facing down, then carefully pull the backing paper off the Pelmform, smoothing it down onto the fabric as you do so.

3 Trim the excess fabric back to 1.5cm (½in). Peel off the paper from the exposed side of the Pelmform in the same way as before, then fold over the seam allowance and press down onto the Pelmform. Turn under a narrow hem on the backing fabric and smooth down onto the Pelmform to line the pelmet.

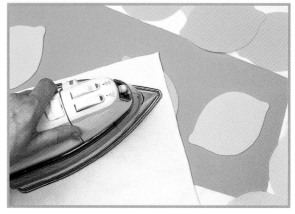

4 Cut out lemon shapes from orange and yellow felt using the template on page 122. Arrange these on the fabric on the front of the pelmet and fix them into position using Bondaweb as described on page 119. Using a glue gun, fix the non-sticky side of the Velcro to the wrong side of the pelmet along the top edge. Stick the opposite edge of the Velcro along the batten, then simply press the pelmet in place.

Drop-in Seat

MANY HOMES HAVE ONE OF THESE CHAIRS WITH A REMOVABLE SEAT, WHICH IS EXTREMELY EASY TO RE-COVER TO MATCH A REDECORATED KITCHEN OR DINING ROOM. THE CHOICE OF FABRIC SETS THE STYLE OF THE CHAIR, WHETHER FORMAL, MODERN OR ELEGANT. IF THE FABRIC HAS A DISTINCT PATTERN, MAKE SURE THAT THIS IS CENTRALIZED ON THE SEAT BEFORE YOU CUT OUT THE FABRIC. IF THE SEAT FITS TIGHTLY INTO THE BASE, YOU WILL NEED TO REMOVE THE OLD COVER BEFORE FITTING THE NEW ONE.

You will need

brown paper or newspaper
paper and dressmaking scissors
fabric the size of the seat plus 8cm (3¼in) border all round
staple gun and staples

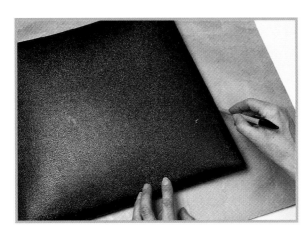

1 Take the seat out of the chair and place on brown paper to make a pattern. Draw round all four sides, then cut out.

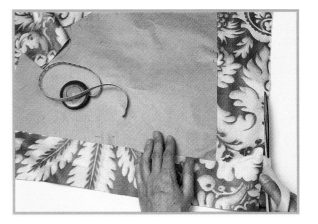

2 Pin the paper pattern to the fabric, making sure that any pattern is centralized, then measure and mark a turning allowance of 8cm (3¼in) all round. Cut out on the marked lines.

BREAKFAST ROOMS

3 Place the chair seat upside down on the wrong side of the fabric. Fold the fabric at the top and bottom over onto the seat and hold in place with a staple. Fold in the corners neatly and staple in place.

4 Trim away any excess fabric, then fold the remaining sides onto the chair back and staple down completely.

▲ **INFORMAL DINING CHAIR**

Gold stars on a cream background make an elegantly simple design, perfect for a kitchen dining room.

▶ **CHILD'S CHAIR**

For a child-like design, we used part of a printed dress fabric with a bold primary-coloured design. We cut this carefully, so that the motif and border fitted on the chair seat.

▶ PERIOD STYLE

A totally different, elegant look can be created on an Art Nouveau chair using bright grass green raw silk, making a style of chair suitable for a formal dining room or as an occasional chair in the living room.

▲ CAFÉ STYLE

To create a continental café type
chair, use a red check or gingham
fabric. For a family breakfast room
choose a wipe-clean fabric.

Canvas Floor Mat

H EAVY-DUTY CANVAS MAKES A BRIGHT AND ATTRACTIVE MAT TO COVER THE WIPE-CLEAN SURFACE OF A KTICHEN OR BATHROOM.

▶ You will need a piece of canvas the size you require for the floor plus 1cm ($^3/_8$in) all round but cut a little extra as canvas shrinks up to 10% when wet. Use a glue gun to make 1cm ($^3/_8$in) hems on all four sides, then apply the stencilled design in the same way as described for the Eyelet Blind on page 50. Once the colours have been fixed, apply several coats of varnish to the canvas, to make the surface more durable.

Squab Cushion

SQUAB CUSHIONS ARE A NEAT AND ATTRACTIVE WAY OF PROVIDING A SOFT SEAT ON A HARD, WOODEN DINING CHAIR. RIBBONS TIE THE SEAT TO THE UPRIGHTS OF THE CHAIR AND COME IN FOR A LOT OF WEAR, SO MAY NEED TO BE REPLACED FAIRLY FREQUENTLY. PLACE A PIECE OF BROWN PAPER OVER THE CHAIR SEAT AND CUT A PATTERN FOR THE FOAM. TAKE THIS WHEN BUYING THE FOAM, SO THAT IT CAN BE CUT TO SHAPE AND MAKE SURE THE FOAM YOU BUY IS FLAME PROOF.

You will need

flame-proofed foam the size of the chair seat and
2.5cm (1in) deep
brown paper or newspaper
fabric to cover back and front plus seam allowances
paper and dressmaking scissors
glue gun and glue sticks
grosgrain ribbon 2.5cm (1in) wide, to go round the
edges of the seat and make ties

1 Make a paper pattern the same shape as the foam but with a seam allowance all round the same depth as the foam, i.e. 2.5cm (1in). Lay the pattern on the fabric and cut out two pieces.

2 Using a glue gun, glue one of the pieces of fabric centrally onto the foam pad, then snip into the seam allowance all round.

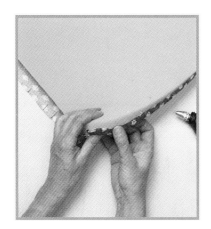

3 Fold the seam allowance onto the side of the foam and glue in place. Repeat for the second piece of fabric, attaching it to the underneath of the foam pad.

4 Glue ribbon all round the sides of the cushion, covering the raw edges, then cut two lengths of ribbon long enough to tie round the back chair leg and to make a bow: ours were 86cm (34in) long. Fold the ribbons in half and glue the centre points to the back corners of the cushion.

HOME OFFICES

IT MAY APPEAR TO BE A CONTRADICTION IN TERMS TO LINK SOFT FURNISHINGS WITH OFFICES, BUT NOT EVERYONE WHO WORKS IN AN OFFICE WANTS A HARD OR CLINICAL ENVIRONMENT. ALSO MANY PEOPLE WORK FROM HOME AND THEIR OFFICE MAY HAVE TO DOUBLE UP AS LIVING ROOM OR SPARE BEDROOM. IN THIS CHAPTER WE SHOW WAYS OF USING SOFT FURNISHINGS TO CREATE FLEXIBLE SPACE TO ACCOMMODATE THIS DUAL FUNCTION. WE HAVE TAKEN AN INEXPENSIVE SHELF UNIT AND MADE A NO-SEW CURTAIN TO COVER ALL OFFICE STATIONERY, THOUGH THE BOX FILES AND RESCUED SHOE BOXES LOOK SO GOOD WITH THEIR FABRIC COVERINGS THAT THE CURTAINS DON'T NEED TO BE DRAWN. AND FOR A SOFA BED, YOU CAN QUICKLY AND EASILY MAKE AN ATTRACTIVE DAYTIME COVER.

Pencil Pleat Curtains

No-sew curtain kits allow curtains to be made with conventional styles of heading tape, though they are not suitable for lined or heavy curtains. To achieve a good result, the adhesive on the tape must be melted into the fabric using a steam iron at the specified temperature. To calculate the fabric required multiply the desired drop by two and add 46cm (18 in). The width is usually two and a half to three times the width of the window (see also page 75).

You will need

light or medium weight fabric
dressmaking scissors
Bondahem and steam iron
no-sew pencil pleat header tape

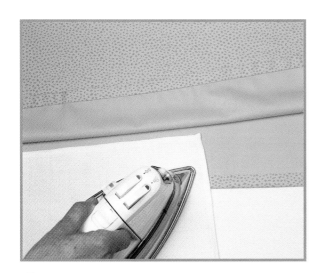

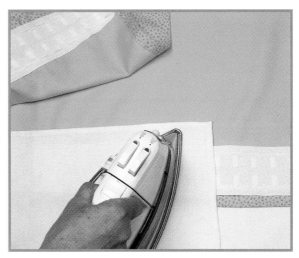

1 If the fabric for each curtain is not wide enough, you will need to Bondahem pieces together to get the required width (see page 40, step 1). At the sides, fold over a 1.5cm (½in) seam allowance and iron Bondahem over the folded edge using a damp cloth. Peel off the paper backing, fold in another 1.5cm (½in) and iron again over a damp cloth.

2 Fold over 1.5cm (½in) at the top of each curtain and Bondahem in place, then iron on the header tape aligned to the top of the folded edge. The header tape has strips of glue running along its wrong side. The iron should be set to the temperature given in the kit you are using.

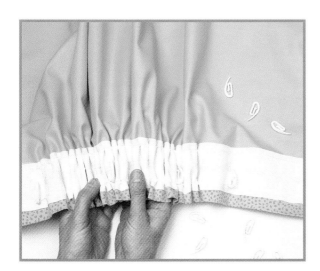

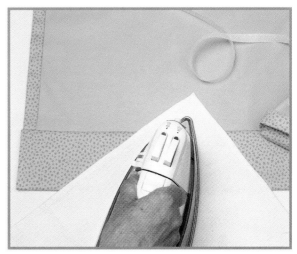

3 Knot the ends of the cords in the heading tape, then pull the cords at one end, adjusting the pleats at the same time, so that they are neatly and evenly spaced, until each curtain is the desired width, i.e. half the width of the window. Knot off the cords. Add curtain hooks at regular intervals.

4 Hang the curtains from the pole or window runner, pin up the hem, remove, then Bondahem in place.

Chest of Drawers

THIS OLD CHEST OF DRAWERS HAS SEEN MANY COATS OF PAINTS, BUT ITS ONCE-FASHIONABLE, DISTRESSED LOOK NOW LOOKS OUT-OF-DATE. WE HAVE GIVEN IT A TOTAL UPDATE BY REPAINTING THE TOP AND SIDES, THEN STAPLING FABRIC TO THE DRAWER FRONTS.

You will need

fine sandpaper
screwdriver
white emulsion
paint brush
pale green emulsion
clear polyurethane varnish (optional)
20cm (8in) each of 4 different fabrics
dressmaking scissors
glue gun and glue sticks
staple gun and staples

HOME OFFICES

1 Remove the drawers. Sand down the carcass of the chest with fine sandpaper. Remove the handles and paint both them and the carcass using white emulsion.

2 When the white emulsion is dry, paint the carcass and the knobs with pale green emulsion. Although we have left the painted wood bare, you could give it a protective coat of clear polyurethane varnish.

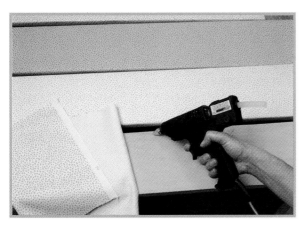

3 Place the drawer front on top of one of the pieces of fabric. Cut the fabric to shape, leaving enough extra all round so that the fabric can be folded back and stapled to the inside. Using a glue gun, add spots of glue to the front of the drawer to hold the fabric in position whilst stapling. Lay over the fabric and press in place. Repeat with the other drawers using the toning fabrics.

4 Holding the fabric firmly and making sure it doesn't distort but remains smooth and flat on the front of the drawer, staple the fabric to the drawer on the inside and underneath. Screw the painted handles back onto the drawer fronts.

Sofa Throw

I F YOUR WORK ROOM HAS TO DOUBLE UP AS A BEDROOM, A SOFA BED IS A GOOD COMPROMISE. TO MAKE IT MORE STYLISH, COVER IT WITH A THROW. CHOOSE A WIDE FURNISHING FABRIC, E.G. 200CM (80IN), SO THAT YOU DO NOT NEED TO JOIN ANY PIECES.

You will need

cream fabric to cover the sofa from front to back with
lots of allowance to tuck the fabric in
dressmaking scissors
glue gun and glue sticks
fringe to go round the outer edge of fabric
108cm (42in) piping cord to fit through the eyelets
instant coffee to dye the cord
marking pencil
eyelet kit and hammer

1 Place the fabric over the sofa, tuck it in round the cushions and make neat folds where the arms meet the seat. Trim the bottom edge, so that it just touches the floor.

2 Turn up a single narrow hem and glue in place, using a glue gun, then pin the fringe round the edge, so that it just overlaps the hem. Glue in place.

3 Gather the fabric neatly over the arms, arranging it in neat pleats. Dye the piping cord by mixing two teaspoons of coffee in a little water and immerse the cord in this. Leave to dry.

4 Mark the position of the two eyelets at the front of the lower arm on each side. These should be placed so that they will be near the edge of the sofa arm once the fabric is gathered in by the cord.

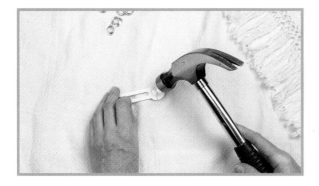

5 Remove the fabric, place on a flat surface and insert the eyelets using a kit. Note, if the fabric is thick you may need to cut a hole to fit the eyelet rather than using the punch.

6 Put the throw back on the sofa and thread the cord through the eyelets, then tie into a bow and knot the ends.

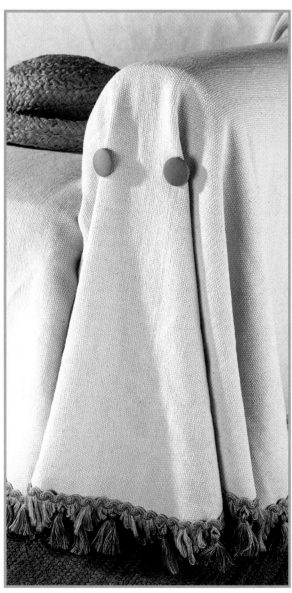

◄ **COORDINATED TRIMMINGS**

Choose a heavyweight, even-weave cotton fabric which is easy to wash. Trim with rust-coloured braid and use a coordinating cord to draw in the fabric over the arms.

► **BUTTONED UP**

As an alternative to the eyelets and bow, use no-sew covered buttons (see page 92) to keep the folds of fabric over the arms in place. Pick out one of the colours from the decorative fringing used round the bottom edge.

Lampshade

TABLE LAMPS IN AN OFFICE PROVIDE SOFTER AMBIENT LIGHT, IN ADDITION TO ANY DESKTOP SPOTLIGHT. THIS IS A VARIATION OF THE LAMPSHADE ON PAGE 89. THE KITS COULD ALSO BE USED TO MAKE COORDINATED HANGING LAMPSHADES.

▶ Make it up in exactly the same way, then, once the rings have been securely fixed in position, glue a bobble trim to the inside lower edge over the bottom ring.

Screen

SCREENS AS AN ITEM OF FURNITURE WENT OUT OF FASHION FOR YEARS BUT HAVE NOW COME INTO VOGUE AGAIN. ALTHOUGH WE HAVE USED OURS IN THE STUDY, IT WOULD BE EQUALLY USEFUL IN A BEDROOM OR BEDSIT WHERE IT COULD CONVENIENTLY HIDE A WASH BASIN OR IN A KITCHEN DINING ROOM WHERE IT COULD SCREEN OFF ONE AREA FROM ANOTHER. ANY DESIGN OF SCREEN WITH SOLID PANELS CAN BE USED AND THIS IS A GOOD TECHNIQUE FOR REJUVENATING AN OLD PIECE.

You will need

brown paper or newspaper to make a pattern
old screen (ours was made from MDF)
paper and dressmaking scissors
lightweight wadding to cover the screen (see method)
glue gun and glue sticks
fabric to cover the screen (see method)
staple gun and staples
braid (see method)

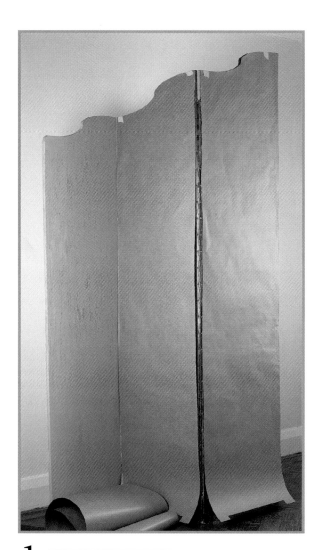

1 Pin brown paper or newspaper onto each panel of the screen to make a pattern. Mark round the outline, then cut each piece to shape.
▷ page 74

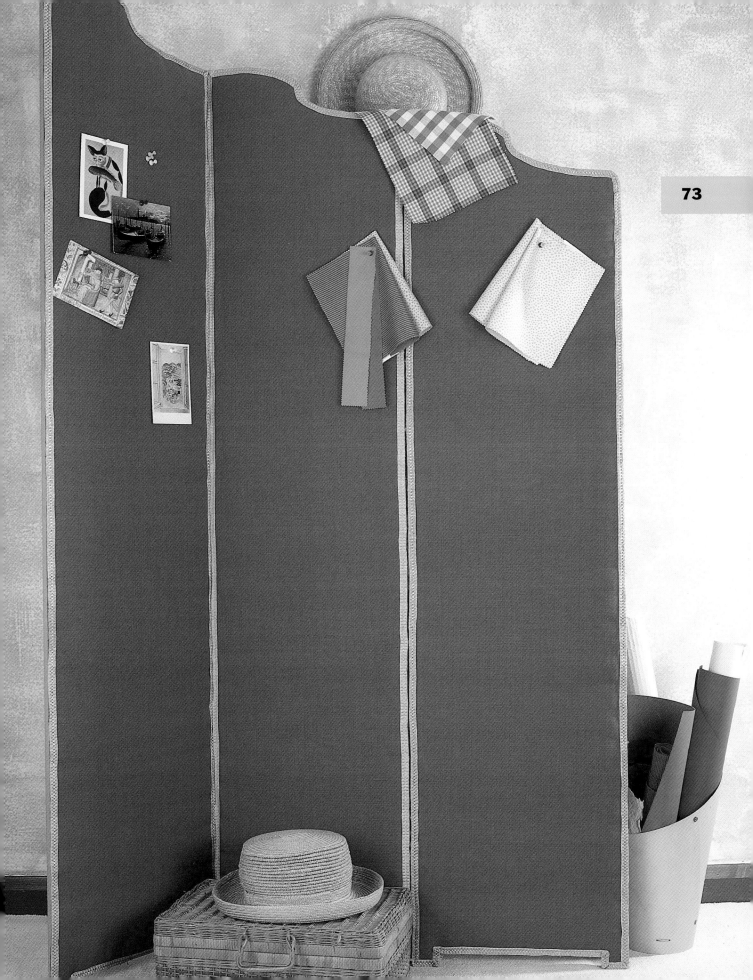

2 Place the pattern pieces side by side to calculate the amount of wadding and fabric you will need. Cut the pieces of wadding 1.5cm (½in) narrower than the pattern. Using a glue gun, stick the wadding centrally to each panel (see left).

3 Cut out the fabric pieces slightly larger than the pattern and staple to the panels as near to the edges of the screen as possible, so that the fabric completely covers the wadding (see above). Trim off the excess fabric close to the sides of the screen.

4 Measure all the way round the edges of each panel of the screen and cut braid to this length, then using a glue gun, stick the braid round the edges, so that it covers up all the staples and raw edges (see left).

Bookshelf Curtains

N O-SEW TECHNIQUES PROVIDE A QUICK AND EASY WAY OF ADDING CURTAINS TO A SET OF SHELVES, MAKING IT AN ATTRACTIVE FEATURE AS WELL AS HIDING AWAY ANY CLUTTER. CHOOSE A LIGHT OR MEDIUM WEIGHT FABRIC, SUCH AS A GLAZED COTTON.

▲ Fit brackets to the top of each of the uprights, then rest a decorative pole on top. Measure one and a half times the width of the pole to find the width of fabric needed and divide by two to find the width of each curtain. For the depth of each curtain, measure from the pole to the floor and add 10cm (4in) for hems at top and bottom. Cut two pieces of fabric to these dimensions. Use Bondahem to turn in the sides and the hems as described on page 65. Place café clips at regular intervals along the top edges of both curtains and attach to the pole.

Storage Boxes

ALL OFFICES, AND HOMES FOR THAT MATTER, NEED STORAGE BOXES. PURPOSE-MADE ONES CAN BE VERY EXPENSIVE, BUT IT IS SIMPLE TO CREATE YOUR OWN, GIVING THE ADDED OPPORTUNITY OF MATCHING THE FABRICS USED TO YOUR INTERIOR DECORATION.

You will need

boxes with separate lids: shoe boxes are ideal and
easily available in many different sizes
brown paper or newspaper and pencil
paper and dressmaking scissors
wadding to cover the lid top
PVA glue or a glue gun and glue sticks
fabric to cover the sides and lid of the box

1 Using the lid as a guide, cut out a paper pattern to the dimensions of the lid plus the depths of the sides inside and out. Mark the corners in a zigzag to cut out excess fabric. Cut wadding to fit the surface of the lid. Glue the wadding to the lid, either with PVA glue or a glue gun.

2 Using the pattern, cut the fabric for the lid. Measure round the outside of the box and add 2.5cm (1in) seam allowance, then measure the depth of the box sides and add 10cm (4in) extra. Cut the remaining fabric to these measurements.

3 Place the fabric for the lid centrally over the wadding, then fold the sides over to the inside of the lid, folding the corners neatly. Glue in position.

4 Place one short side of the fabric for the box vertically on one of the corners of the box, so that it overlaps by 2cm (¾in) at the top and 8cm (3¼in) at the bottom. Wrap the fabric round the box, fold in the seam allowance on the opposite short side and glue in place. Fold the surplus to the inside at the top of the box and glue down. Fold the surplus onto the base of the box. Trim away the excess at the corners and glue down.

Magazine Files

CARDBOARD FILES, SUCH AS THE ONES USED HERE, CAN BE OBTAINED FROM MOST STATIONERY SHOPS. THEY ARE VERY GOOD VALUE BUT EXCEEDINGLY DULL. BY USING UP FABRIC REMNANTS YOU CAN MAKE BRIGHT AND CHEERFUL FILES TO MATCH THE ROOM SCHEME. THEY'RE VITAL FOR OFFICE PAPERS AND A GREAT ACCESSORY FOR THE KITCHEN TO HOLD RECIPE TEARSHEETS, LETTERS, BILLS, ETC.

You will need

80 x 44cm (31 x 17 $\frac{1}{2}$in) fabric for each file

cardboard files

PVA glue and brush

cutting board

craft knife or dressmaking scissors

water-based paint and brush in chosen colour (optional)

thin cord or coloured string

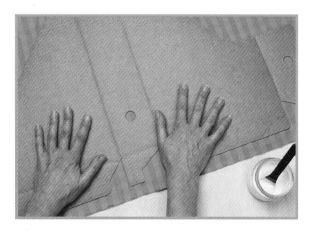

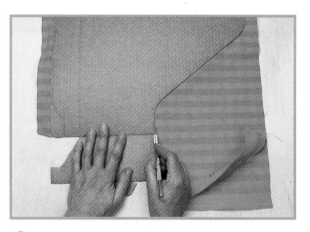

1 Cut a piece of fabric slightly larger than the file when it is opened up. Brush the outside of the opened-out file with PVA glue. Place the file, glued side down, on top of the wrong side of the fabric and press them together so there are no wrinkles. Leave to dry. Place a weight, such as a heavy book, on top of the file to stop it from warping.

2 When the fabric is dry, place on a cutting board and, using a craft knife, cut away the excess fabric. You can use scissors, but a craft knife gives a neater finish.

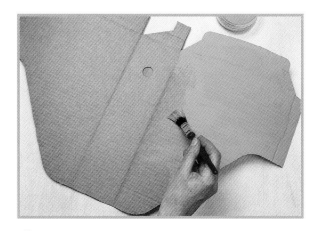

3 As an option, paint the back or inside of the file before you put it together. Emulsion sample pots are good for this.

4 If the back of the file has a hole in it, cut away the fabric with a craft knife, then, using PVA glue, fix string or cord round the outer edges of the file.

Picture Frame

PICTURE FRAMES ARE ONE OF THOSE HOME ACCESSORIES OF WHICH ONE CAN NEVER HAVE TOO MANY. YOU CAN GIVE THEM A TAILORED LOOK, SUCH AS THE ONE SHOWN, OR MAKE THEM SOFTER LOOKING BY ADDING WADDING BEFORE COVERING WITH FABRIC. IT IS BEST TO CHOOSE A FRAME WITH A WIDE FRONT, SO THAT LOTS OF FABRIC IS SHOWING FOR MAXIMUM IMPACT.

You will need

purchased frame
paper to make a template and pencil
ruler
enough fabric to cover the front of the frame plus a little extra for turnings
paper and dressmaking scissors
glue gun and glue sticks
ribbon trim

1 Place paper over one short side of the frame and mark the points of the inner and outer edges, then cut out. Place on another piece of paper and extend the pattern by 1.5cm (½in) on the inner edge and 5cm (2in) on the outer. Repeat for the longer side. Cut out the extended templates. If the frame is square, you will only need one template.

2 Place the extended templates on top of the fabric and cut two short sides and two long sides.

3 Place the fabric flat over the frame, matching diagonal lines and corners. Using the glue gun, stick the fabric in place on the frame. Fold the overlap to the back and glue these in place.

4 Cut pieces of ribbon the length of the mitre plus 7.5cm (3in). Glue the ribbon centrally over the mitres to cover the raw edges of the fabric, fold the excess to the back and glue down.

BEDROOMS

THIS CHAPTER OFFERS A VARIETY OF STYLES, FROM SIMPLE BUT ELEGANT THROUGH ROMANTIC TO MINIMALIST, ALL CREATED USING NO-SEW TECHNIQUES. THERE IS A WARDROBE CURTAIN AND A RADIATOR COVER MADE FROM GATHERED FABRICS; A SIMPLE LAMPSHADE; TWO TYPES OF QUICK AND SIMPLE CURTAINS; A WOODEN SHELVING UNIT MADE SOFTER AND PRETTIER WITH A GINGHAM COVER; A FOUR POSTER BED SWATHED IN MUSLIN AND COVERED IN A VERY BEAUTIFUL TOILE DE JOUY AND, FOR A CONTEMPORARY GUEST BEDROOM, A FUTON HAS BEEN GIVEN A DENIM COVER WITH A STRIKING EYELET AND CORD FASTENING.

Futon Cover

FUTONS ARE PERFECT PIECES OF FURNITURE FOR SMALL ROOMS OR ROOMS WITH A DUAL FUNCTION: THEY TURN FROM SEAT TO BED WITH THE MINIMUM OF FUSS. THIS SIMPLE COVER MADE USING TWO FABRICS LACED TOGETHER WITH CORD CROSSES, MARRIES A WESTERN FABRIC WITH AN EASTERN THEME IN THE BEST CONTEMPORARY MANNER. IT'S PILED HIGH WITH NO-SEW CUSHIONS WHICH COULD ALSO SERVE AS PILLOWS.

You will need

denim or other wide fabric to cover the futon front and back plus 25cm
(10in) seam allowance all round
marking pencil and ruler
Bondahem and iron
eyelet kit and hammer
piping cord the correct width for the eyelets, two and a half times the
distance round all four sides

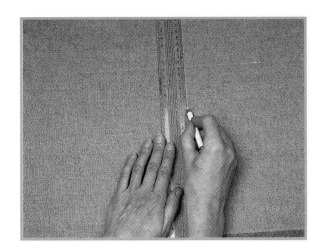

1 Cut two pieces of fabric to fit the front and back of the futon and allowing a 25cm (10in) border all round. On one of the pieces, measure 25cm (10in) from each edge on the reverse side and mark with a contrast coloured pencil.

2 At each corner, fold in the point up to the marked edges. Iron Bondahem just inside the marked line on one side, stopping at the folded-over corner point. Fold over the edge by 12.5cm (5in), remove the paper backing from the Bondahem and iron in position. Repeat on the other three sides, to give mitred corners and a 12.5cm (5in) border all round.

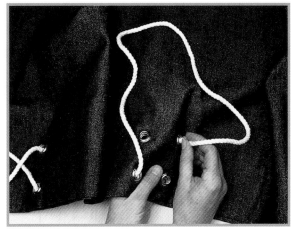

3 Mark the positions of the eyelets on the reverse side of the border. Each set of four should be 2.5cm (1in) from the folded edge and 5cm (2in) apart. Start with a set of four in each corner. The distance between the sets depends on the length of your futon but keep them fairly close together, so that they keep the two covers securely fixed. Using the eyelet kit and a hammer, insert the eyelets.

4 Repeat steps one to three with the second piece of fabric, making sure that the eyelet holes are in exactly the same positions. Place the two pieces, wrong sides together, then thread piping cord through the eyelets through both layers to form crosses on the front of the cover. Use a separate piece of cord for each side and knot the ends underneath.

Headboard

A PADDED BEDHEAD MAKES A COMFORTABLE HEAD REST. USE A SIMPLE PADDED BOARD, COVERED IN CALICO. THE PADDED PART SITS ABOVE THE MATTRESS, THE UNPADDED SECTION AGAINST IT. CHOOSE A FABRIC WHICH DOES NOT NEED COMPLICATED MATCHING. MAKE SURE THAT WHEN THE FABRIC IS APPLIED IT IS NOT PULLED AT AN ANGLE BUT GOES WITH THE STRAIGHT OF THE GRAIN. MEASURE THE WIDTH AND DEPTH OF THE PADDED PART OF THE HEADBOARD AT THE LONGEST POINTS. ADD AN OVERLAP ALL ROUND OF 20CM (8IN).

You will need

simple padded board
fabric for front and back of headboard, either
matching or contrasting (see method)
dressmaking scissors
staple gun and staples
chalk or marking pencil

1 Cut the fabric to the required dimensions (see opposite), then pin centrally to the front of the board. Staple the fabric to the front underneath the padded section, then pull the fabric to the back of the board at the top and sides. Staple in position, pleating the excess neatly at the corners.

2 Measure the unpadded front at the base of headboard adding 20cm (8in) overlap all round. Cut the fabric to these measurements and fold over the allowance on one long edge. Place the folded edge underneath the padded section, matching checks or patterns. Pin, then staple in position. ▷ *page 88*

BEDROOMS

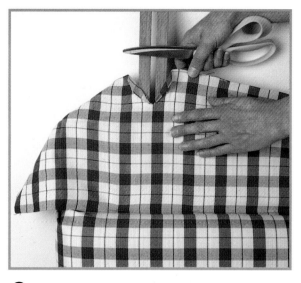

3 Pull the rest of the fabric to the back of the board making a vertical cut into the fabric to accommodate the legs. Staple in place, pleating at the corners.

4 Measure the width and depth of the back of the headboard at the longest points. Add an overlap all round of 10cm (4in). Cut the backing fabric to these measurements. Place in position centrally on the back of the board and mark round the edges of the board with chalk. Pin in place.

5 Trim off the excess leaving a 1.5cm (½in) seam allowance.

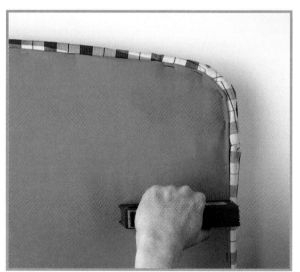

6 Turn under the seam allowance all round and staple into place at the back of the headboard, covering all raw edges.

Table Lampshade

THIS CHARMING LAMPSHADE IS MADE USING A KIT WHICH CONSISTS OF FIXINGS AND A PRECUT SHADE MADE FROM A HEAT RESISTANT PVC WITH A STICKY BACKING. CLOSE WEAVE FABRICS ARE THE BEST AS THEY DO NOT HOLD DUST; USE ANYTHING FROM SILK TO COTTON OR POLYESTER. THESE KITS ARE DESIGNED WITH SAFETY IN MIND, SO THE SHADE IS HELD A LONG WAY FROM THE BULB. HOWEVER, ALWAYS USE A LOW WATTAGE BULB. FABRIC FIRE RETARDANT IS AVAILABLE FROM THEATRICAL SUPPLIERS.

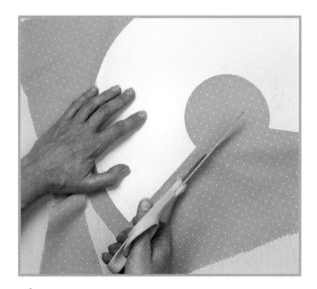

You will need

fabric to cover the precut shade plus 5 to 8cm (2 to 3in) extra all round

lampshade kit

dressmaking and small scissors

glue gun and glue sticks

pegs or paper clips

superglue

1 Iron the fabric and place right side down on the work surface. Place the precut shade on top, adhesive side down. Carefully pull off the backing and smooth down onto the fabric. Turn over and smooth out any wrinkles. Cut round the shape leaving a 2.5cm (1in) seam allowance. ▷ *page 90*

B E D R O O M S

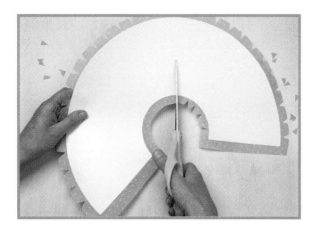

2 Make notches at regular intervals on circular edges of the inside and outside. The notching makes it easier to manipulate the fabric and gives a smoother finish.

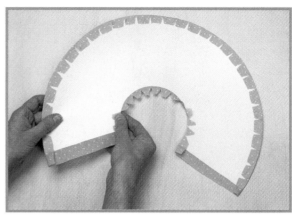

3 Fold the notched edges down onto the shade and glue into place using a glue gun.

4 Fold in one of the straight edges and glue into position. Cut off the other close to the backing.

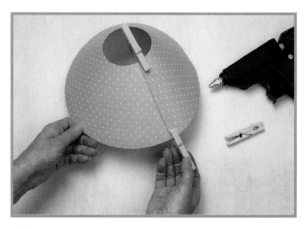

5 Form the shape into a shade placing the folded straight edge over the cut edge with a 1cm (⅜in) overlap. Glue and hold into position until dry with paper clips or pegs.

6 Using superglue, stick the inner and outer rings into position on the inside of the shade and hold these with pegs until dry.

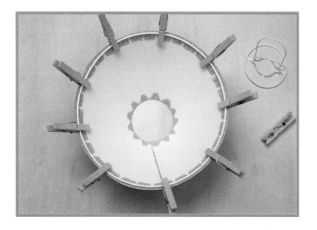

Tab-top Curtains

THESE CURTAINS SHOW A VARIATION ON THE LIVING ROOM CURTAINS ON PAGE 14. HERE THE TAB-TOP HEADING IS MADE USING A KIT WHICH INCLUDES BUTTONS TO FASTEN THE TABS TO THE CURTAIN. THE TABS COULD BE MADE IN A CONTRASTING FABRIC FOR ADDED IMPACT. FOR THE CURTAINS YOU WILL NEED ONE AND A HALF TIMES THE WIDTH OF THE WINDOW AND THE LENGTH OF THE DROP PLUS 30CM (12IN) FOR HEMS, TOP AND BOTTOM. TURN IN THE SIDES WITH BONDAHEM AND MAKE THE TOP TURNING AND BOTTOM HEM IN THE SAME WAY, THEN MAKE UP THE TABS AND BUTTONS FROM THE KIT AS DESCRIBED OPPOSITE.

You will need

fabric for curtain, tabs and button

tab-top kit

dressmaking scissors

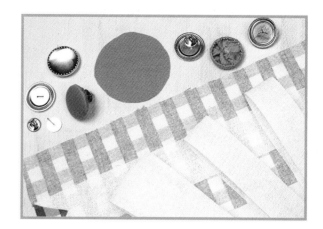

1 Cut out a circle of fabric using the template given. Pull the fabric over the button and tuck it into the middle using the teeth to hold it in place. Make the tabs following the kit instructions.

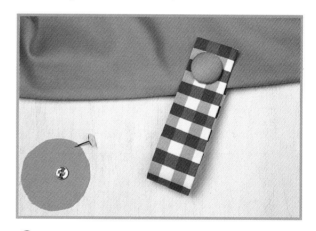

2 Push the pin through the back plate of the button, then place the back plate over the button so that the pin protrudes. Apply pressure to snap the back plate in place. To attach the tab to the curtain, fold the tab in half and place in position at the top of the curtain. Push the pin of the button through all layers and fasten at the back with the butterfly clip.

B E D R O O M S

Eyelet Curtains

▲ RED GINGHAM BOW TIES

Make separate ties through each eyelet with wire-edged ribbon. The wire edges hold the ribbon in shape, preventing the bows from flopping over.

▲ BLUE AND WHITE TIES

In complete contrast to the gingham bows, using two grosgrain ribbons knotted together in smart white and blue gives a much more formal, tailored look.

EYELETS CAN BE USED TO TURN A PLAIN PIECE OF FABRIC INTO A CURTAIN. AS THE VARIATIONS SHOW, A GREAT VARIETY OF LOOKS MAY BE ACHIEVED THIS WAY. USE THIS METHOD FOR CURTAINS WHICH WILL NOT BE USED FREQUENTLY, AS THE FRICTION ON THE RIBBON WILL EVENTUALLY CAUSE IT TO WEAR OUT. THE GINGHAM FABRIC USED FOR THESE CURTAINS HAS A SLIGHTLY AGED FEEL WITH ITS SOFT CREAM RATHER THAN WHITE BACKGROUND TO CONTRAST WITH THE PALE BLUE.

▶ The basic curtain is made in the same way as described on page 16. A row of eyelets is then inserted along the top, ribbon is threaded through each eyelet and over the curtain rail. The ribbon used is a grosgrain, which is stronger than satin. It is slightly wider than the eyelets, which helps to prevent it from slipping.

elf Cover

A PLAIN WOODEN SHELVING UNIT, WAIST HIGH WITH THREE SHELVES, HAS BEEN CONVERTED INTO A STORE CUPBOARD FOR LINEN, CLOTHES AND OTHER NECESSARY BUT UNTIDY BEDROOM BITS AND PIECES. A FABRIC COVERING HAS BEEN STAPLED TO THE SIDES AND A DETACHABLE SCREEN ADDED TO THE FRONT TO HIDE AWAY ANY CLUTTER.

You will need

wooden shelving unit (this one is 90.5cm wide x
70.5cm high/35½ x 27¾in)
2m (2¼yds) cotton fabric, 90cm (36in) wide
dressmaking scissors
masking tape
staple gun and staples
glue gun and glue sticks
90cm (36in) length of stick-on Velcro
Bondahem and iron

1 Cut two pieces of fabric, 80 x 40cm (32 x 16in), for the sides of the unit. Cut another piece, 96.5 x 77cm (38 x 30⅓in), for the screen. Place one of the side pieces over the side of the top shelf, allowing it to hang over the top. Fold the corner neatly at the top and hold in place with masking tape.

2 Wrap the fabric smoothly round the upright struts and staple into position along the top front edge and at the back of the struts, adjusting and snipping as necessary. Repeat with the other side of the shelf unit.

B E D R O O M S

3 Using the glue gun, attach one half of the Velcro to the top front edge of the shelving unit, along its complete length. Take the remaining piece of fabric and check for fit over the front of the shelves. Mark the seams all round, trim to 1.5cm (½in), then use Bondahem to fix in place.

4 Glue the opposing length of Velcro along the top edge of the wrong side of the screen fabric and attach to the shelving unit. Note, this leaves the top shelf uncovered. You could make a simple cover for it if liked. Cut to size with seam allowances and Bondahem the sides to neaten.

Radiator Cover

A NEAT WAY TO COVER A RADIATOR IS TO MAKE A WOODEN FRAME SIMILAR TO A WINDOW FRAME, THEN ADD PLEATED FABRIC TO THE INSIDE. A LOCAL CARPENTER WILL BE ABLE TO MAKE THE FRAME, WHICH CAN THEN BE PAINTED TO MATCH YOUR ROOM DECORATION. THE FRAME CAN BE REMOVED IN THE WINTER TO GET FULL BENEFIT OF THE HEAT.

You will need

fabric to cover the radiator – this will depend on how full you want the radiator curtains to be: for a full cover, use twice the width of the radiator times the drop; for less full, use one and a half times the width
staple gun and staples
grosgrain ribbon twice the width of each radiator door plus 10cm (4in) for turnings
glue gun and glue sticks

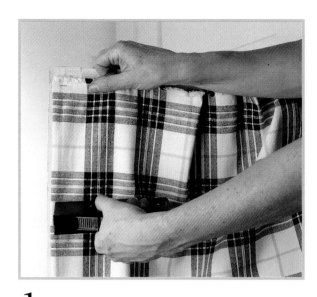

1 Cut two pieces of fabric, one for each door. Turn under one short edge and staple to the lefthand inside edge of the door, so that the right side of the fabric faces out.

2 Working along the top of the door from the inside, make small pleats in the fabric to simulate gathers and staple into position along the inside top of the frame. Check the effect from the front and adjust if necessary. Staples can be removed using a screwdriver.

3 When the fabric is evenly gathered at the top, repeat the process at the bottom, pulling the fabric taut and making sure that the pleats are vertical.

4 Turn under the allowance at one end of the grosgrain ribbon and, using the glue gun, attach to the top left edge of the fabric. Continue glueing the ribbon over the raw edges of the pleated fabric, turning under the allowance at the righthand end and glueing in place. Repeat at the bottom of the curtain. Attach the second curtain in the same way.

Wardrobe Curtain

▲ To make a curtain for a deep frame such as this wardrobe door, choose a lightweight fabric which can be pulled taut more easily and will not be too heavy for the door.

A NY DOOR WITH A WIRED OR GLASS FRONT CAN BE COVERED IN FABRIC IN THE SAME WAY AS FOR THE RADIATOR COVER. THESE PRETTY FABRIC COVERS ARE IDEAL FOR BEDROOM CUPBOARDS, WHERE YOU DO NOT WANT THE CONTENTS TO BE ON DISPLAY.

BEDROOMS

Shaped Chair Cushion

MAKE AN INSTANT CUSHION FOR A SHAPED CHAIR SEAT SIMPLY BY FOLDING FABRIC OVER A FOAM PAD AND USING EYELETS AT THE BACK TO HOLD IT IN POSITION. FOAM SUPPLIERS WILL CUT A PIECE TO SHAPE IF YOU TAKE ALONG A PAPER PATTERN. MAKE SURE THAT IT IS FIRE RETARDANT. THIS PAD IS 5CM (2IN) DEEP. FOR THE FABRIC MEASURE THE FRONT OF THE CUSHION AND ADD 15CM (6IN) OVERLAP ALL ROUND.

1 Wrap the fabric round the pad, pleat the excess neatly at the back and pin. Mark the position of the eyelets, one on each pleat. Remove the fabric and insert the eyelets through each pleat.

2 Replace the fabric round the cushion and trim off the excess. Remove the pins. Thread thin eyelet cord through the holes, pull up loosely and knot to hold the cushion cover in position.

Four Poster Bed

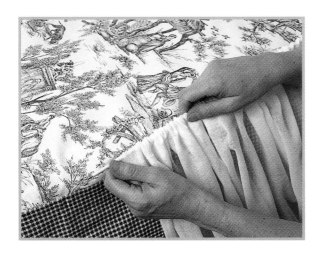

EVERYONE'S DREAM OF ROMANCE MUST BE THE FOUR POSTER BED. WE HAVE TAKEN MUSLIN, THE MOST HUMBLE OF FABRICS, AND USED IT TO CREATE A FLOATY ROMANTIC PICTURE. THE LIGHTNESS OF MUSLIN ALSO MAKES IT PERFECT FOR HANGING FROM COVERED WIRE; A HEAVIER FABRIC WOULD TEND TO SAG. BY USING DOUBLE THE WIDTH OF THE SIDES OF THE BED YOU CAN CREATE FULL CURTAINS.

You will need

muslin (see below)
dressmaking scissors
Bondahem the same width as the measured fabric
iron
10 cup hooks
plastic-covered wire to fit the width of the four sides
with an eye ring at each end

1 Measure the width of each side of the bed and double this measurement. Divide this by the width of the muslin to find the number of lengths. Measure the drop from the top of the cross beams to the floor and add 6cm (2½in) seam allowance to give the measurement of each length. Multiply this by the number of lengths to give the total length of fabric required. Cut the fabric into the lengths measured. At the top of each piece of fabric, fold over 5cm (2in) and Bondahem along the raw edge to make a channel to take the wire. Screw the cup hooks into the inner corners of the four poster and one in the middle of each of the two longer sides. Cut the wire to fit each side, stretching it a little between the hooks. Thread each curtain onto the wire and hook up (see left).

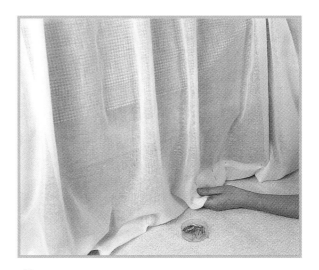

2 Pin up the hems on each length of muslin while it is hanging in place. The fabric should rest on the floor rather than just above it (see above). Remove the curtains and iron on Bondahem as described on page 16 to make the hems.

B E D R O O M S

▲ FOUR POSTER TIEBACKS

You can embellish and enhance the romance of the muslin drapes by pulling back the curtains with beautiful ties. Here a length of grade-dyed muslin (see page 11) has simply been tied round the curtains at the foot of the bed, taken up to the cross beam draped in a loop and brought down to the opposite side to make a second tieback. You could also use short lengths of plain white muslin to make big bow tiebacks for a less feminine but still highly romantic effect.

Toile de Jouy Bedcover

THE CONTRAST BETWEEN THE RURAL

SCENE ON THIS TOILE DE JOUY

BEDCOVER AND THE SMALL CRISP GINGHAM

CHECK USED TO BORDER IT GIVES A

CONTEMPORARY TOUCH TO A CLASSIC FABRIC.

▲ You will need enough fabric to cover the bed in the main fabric. For the border fabric you will need a piece 70cm (27½in) longer than the cover fabric and 140cm (55in) wide. This will give a doubled border 15cm (6in) wide. The border is attached in exactly the same way as for the Tablecloth on page 40.

CHILDREN'S ROOMS

W E HAVE CHOSEN A SEA THEME FOR THIS ROOM, SINCE IT IS A POPULAR THEME WITH ALL CHILDREN. HOWEVER, YOU COULD CHOOSE A DIFFERENT THEME SUCH AS FAIRIES, ZOO ANIMALS, JUNGLES, THE CIRCUS OR SPACE EXPLORATION. JUST USE OUR GUIDELINES FOR MAKING UP THE PROJECTS. WHEN MAKING ANYTHING FOR CHILDREN, MAKE SURE THAT ALL PIECES ARE SECURE AND CANNOT COME LOOSE WITH THE DANGER THAT THEY MAY BE SWALLOWED. ALL THE IMAGES USED HERE ARE AVAILABLE AS TEMPLATES AT THE END OF THE BOOK. IF YOU CHOOSE A DIFFERENT THEME, LOOK IN CHILDREN'S BOOKS FOR SIMPLE, STYLIZED SHAPES: THESE HAVE A GREATER VISUAL IMPACT AND ARE EASIER TO CUT AND APPLY.

Children's Curtains

Small windows are perfect for no-sew curtains made with a simple heading tape kit. The fabric is medium weight but because the windows are not deep, they will not be too heavy for this method.

◄ For the curtain fabric, you will need one and a half times the width of the curtain and the length plus 46cm (18in) for turnings. For the motifs, you will need felt fabric in white, green, orange and pale blue plus Bondaweb. Make up the curtains following the method on page 64. Trace the designs from pages 125 and 126 and work out how many waves and boats will fit your curtain widths, then appliqué to the finished curtains as described for the bedhead opposite. Iron the sails in place first, then the bottom of the boats and finally the waves.

Children's Bedhead

T HESE THREE SHIPS ARE ALL
SLIGHTLY DIFFERENT IN SIZE AND
ARE DESIGNED TO FIT THE FRONT OF THE
HEADBOARD. THE BASIC METHOD FOR
COVERING THE FRONT AND BACK OF A
PADDED HEADBOARD IN FABRIC IS
DESCRIBED ON PAGE 86.

▲ For this version you will also need white, green and orange felt plus Bondaweb for the appliqué shapes. Pin the bedhead fabric temporarily in position. Trace the designs for the ships given on page 125, then draw round them onto the backing paper of the webbing. Cut out the shapes. Position these on the bedhead fabric above the level of the mattress. Mark the positions. Remove the fabric, then, using the green for the flags, white for the sails and orange for the boat, iron on the webbing shapes to the felts and cut out. Remove the paper backing and iron the ship shapes in position, then continue with the basic bedhead method.

Wave-edged Pelmet

T HE PELMET USED HERE IS A READY-
FORMED SHAPE MADE FROM MDF.
YOU COULD USE A MORE CONVENTIONAL
SHAPE AND DECORATE IT IN THE SAME
WAY. YOU WILL NEED TO CUT THE PELMET
TO FIT THE WINDOW BEFORE YOU START
AND FIT BRACKETS TO HOLD IT IN PLACE.
WE HAVE COVERED IT IN A LIGHTWEIGHT FELT, WHICH HAS A GOOD
STRONG COLOUR, IS NON-FRAYING AND MATCHES THE WAVE DESIGN ON
THE CURTAINS.

You will need

MDF pelmet
blue felt slightly larger than the pelmet
dressmaking scissors
glue gun and glue sticks
craft knife
tracing paper and pencil
small pieces of yellow, green, orange, red, black and
white felt for the motifs

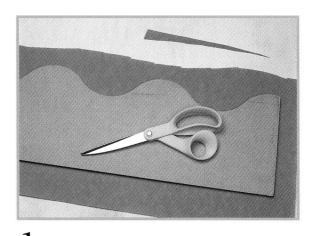

1 Cut the blue felt roughly to shape slightly larger than the pelmet.

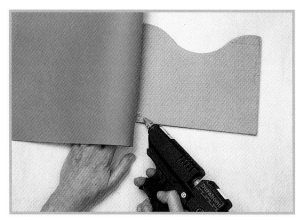

2 Stick the felt firmly to the front of the pelmet using the glue gun.

CHILDREN'S ROOMS

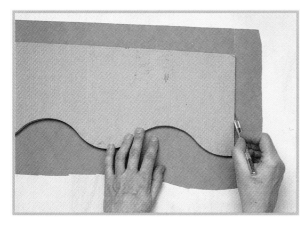

3 Turn the pelmet over and, using a sharp craft knife, trim the fabric close to the edge of the pelmet all the way round.

4 Make paper tracings of the fish, starfish and boat motifs from pages 124 and 125. Cut out and use as templates to cut the designs from felt using the colours shown. Glue gun these into position on the pelmet.

Toy Box

Transform a plain toy box by adding canvas painted with a mottled design and decorated with appliqué shapes. As with many of the no-sew pieces, this doesn't have to be a permanent change. You can change the canvas covering either by removing the old one, easing it off with a knife or glueing a new cover on top.

You will need

canvas to cover the top and sides of the toy chest
including a 5cm (2in) seam allowance all round plus
another 50cm (20in) for appliqué shapes
dressmaking scissors
acrylic paints: blue (two shades), green (two shades),
orange, yellow, red and white
stencil brush to apply the paint
glue gun and glue sticks
tracing paper and pencil
fray stop or PVA glue
grosgrain ribbon or another robust ribbon suitable to
go round the four edges of the lid

1 Measure the four sides and lid of the toy box, then cut five pieces of canvas to fit, allowing approximately 5cm (2in) extra for seam allowance and shrinkage.

2 Stipple each piece with scattered patches of one of the green paints. Leave to dry, then apply the second shade of green and the two blues in the same way.

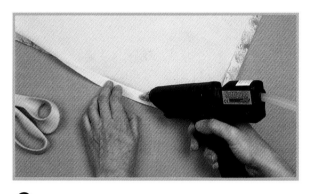

3 When the canvas is completely dry, fold in the pieces to fit each side and the lid and trim the allowance back to 1.5cm (½in). Using a glue gun, attach each piece to the appropriate part of the box.

4 Trace off the seaweed, fish and starfish templates from pages 124 and 125. Pin to the remaining canvas and draw round. Cut roughly to shape and stipple the surface with paints as shown in the photograph.

5 Apply fray stop to the outline on the back of each shape and rub in. Alternatively, paint on PVA glue using a fine paint brush. Leave to dry, then cut out each shape.

6 Arrange the seaweed at the bottom of each side and the fish and starfish above, then glue gun them onto the box. Glue the ribbon all round the edges of the lid.

Appliquéed Bedcover

THIS IS THE EASIEST WAY OF MAKING A DECORATIVE BEDCOVER FOR A CHILD. ALL YOU HAVE TO DO IS APPLIQUÉ DESIGNS ONTO A PURCHASED COVER. DEPENDING ON HOW SUBSTANTIAL YOU WANT IT TO BE, USE EITHER A COTTON BEDSPREAD OR SIMPLY A SHEET.

▲ Make paper tracings of the flying fish using the template on page 122. Place the cover over the bed and pin the tracings in position. You could place them round the edge of the bed as shown in the photograph on page 106 or all over for a really busy design. Mark the positions with pins or chalk, then cut out the required number of fish from a non-fraying fabric, such as felt. Use Bondaweb to bond the designs onto the cover, as described on page 119.

Chest of Drawers

THIS LIVELY DESIGN HAS BEEN USED TO RENOVATE AN OLD PIECE OF FURNITURE TO MAKE IT PERFECT FOR A CHILD'S OWN ROOM.

▼ This is a variation on the method used for covering the toybox on page 113. Here the canvas has been cut to fit the fronts of the drawers without seam allowance. It has been attached to the drawers using a glue gun and the designs have been painted on and outlined with a gold acrylic paint.

Children's Cushions

THESE CUSHIONS ARE MADE FROM A NON-FRAYING, WASHABLE FABRIC. THEY ARE QUICK TO MAKE, SO YOU CAN MAKE TWO OR THREE IN VERY LITTLE TIME. ALTHOUGH WE HAVE CHOSEN A CIRCLE YOU COULD, OF COURSE, MAKE THEM SQUARE, OBLONG OR EVEN CAR OR TRAIN-SHAPED. MAKE SURE ALL APPLIQUÉ PIECES ARE FIRMLY STUCK DOWN.

You will need

for each cushion:
40cm (16in) square of wadding
dressmaking scissors
two squares of 40cm (16in) blue non-fraying fabric
glue gun and glue sticks
tracing paper and pencil
30cm (12in) white, 13cm (5in) yellow, 18cm (7in) orange, 27cm (11in) navy blue non-fraying fabrics for the designs
pinking shears

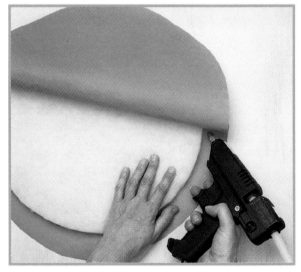

1 Use a large circle, such as a dinner plate or dustbin lid, to cut out a circle of wadding, then cut two pieces of non-fraying fabric 2.5cm (1in) wider than the wadding.

2 Place the wadding on top of one piece of fabric and glue gun in two or three places to hold in position. Glue gun the front firmly to the back, wrong sides together, round the edges with the wadding in the centre.

CHILDREN'S ROOMS

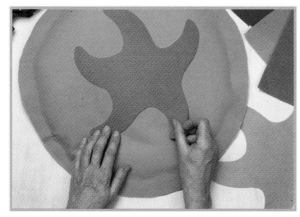

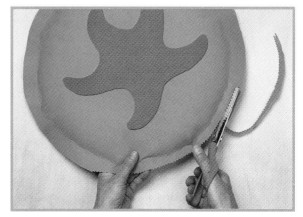

3 Trace off the chosen design from the motifs on pages 124, 125 and 126. Cut out in the chosen contrast colour, then arrange on the cushion. Fix in place using a glue gun.

4 Make a neat edge all the way round the cushion using a pair of pinking shears.

Room Tidy

THIS HANGING HIDES AN UNSIGHTLY DOORWAY BUT YOU CAN MAKE THE SAME THING TO HANG ON THE BACK OF A DOOR OR FROM THE SIDE OF A BUNK BED. IT COULD HAVE LOTS MORE POCKETS OR JUST THREE AS HERE. THE POCKETS ARE NOT STRONG ENOUGH TO TAKE ANYTHING HEAVY BUT ARE PERFECT FOR TIDYING AWAY PAPERS OR SMALL TOYS.

You will need

tracing paper and pencil
Bondaweb and iron
dressmaking scissors
scraps of red, white and blue felt to make pockets
pinking shears
fabric to cover the door (or wherever you want to hang it) plus 1.5cm (½in) seam allowance at the sides and bottom and 6cm (2 ½in) at the top.
Bondahem
eyelet kit and hammer
piping cord to thread through the eyelets
2 cup hooks with a slightly larger diameter than the doweling
piece of painted doweling
glue gun and glue sticks

1 Make tracings of the life belt pieces on page 123. Draw round these templates onto the paper backing of the Bondaweb to make three life belts. Cut out. Place the circles on the white felt and the segments on the red felt. Iron in place. Cut out the shapes from the felt. Cut out three square pockets from the blue felt using pinking shears. It is best not to make these too big, ours are 20cm (8in) square.

2 Peel off the paper backing from the white circles and place in the centre of the blue pockets. Iron in position over a damp cloth. Peel off the paper backing from the red segments and place in position on the white circles. Iron in position over a damp cloth as before to complete the life belt.

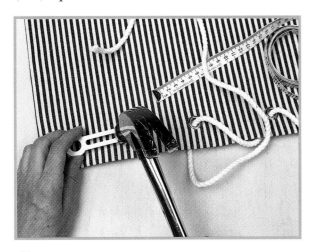

3 Fold over the 1.5cm (½in) seam allowance at the sides of the hanging fabric and Bondahem in place. Fold over 6cm (2½in) at the top and Bondahem in place. Mark along the top of the fabric at regular intervals 2cm (1in) down from the folded edge, then, using the eyelet kit, insert a row of eyelets at these points. Thread the cord in and out of the eyelets, leaving extra at both ends.

4 Screw the cup hooks in position. Thread the doweling through the cord loops and hang from the hooks. Knot the cord at either end and trim off the excess. Pin the pockets in position on the hanging and pin the hem, then take down and using the glue gun, glue the pockets in position. Iron a double hem at the bottom of the hanging and secure with Bondahem.

Director's Chair

PEOPLE OFTEN HAVE ONE OF THESE CHAIRS LYING AROUND THEIR HOME. THE PROBLEM IS THAT THE FABRIC USUALLY WEARS OUT LONG BEFORE THE FRAME. THIS NO-SEW TECHNIQUE IS IDEAL FOR REPLACING THE COVERS.

You will need

brown paper or newspaper
paper and dressmaking scissors
firmly woven fabric for the seat and the back of the
chair plus 1.5cm (½in) seam allowance at top and
bottom and 10cm (4in) at the sides
glue gun and glue sticks

Note : Director's chairs differ slightly in the way in which they are constructed, some have channels at the sides of the chair some do not. You may need to staple the seat in position.

1 Remove the original covers from the chair and open out the channels made for the back and seat supports. Draw round the pieces onto the paper, adding a 1.5cm (½in) seam allowance all round.

2 Cut out the paper patterns, then pin them onto the new fabric and cut out.

3 Turn under the seam allowance along the front and back edges of the seat cover and the top and bottom edges of the seat back. Using the glue gun, glue in place.

4 Fold in the sides of the back cover to make a channel wide enough to fit the seat uprights. Glue gun these into position. Repeat with the sides of the chair.

Templates

If necessary, enlarge designs on a
photocopier to size required.

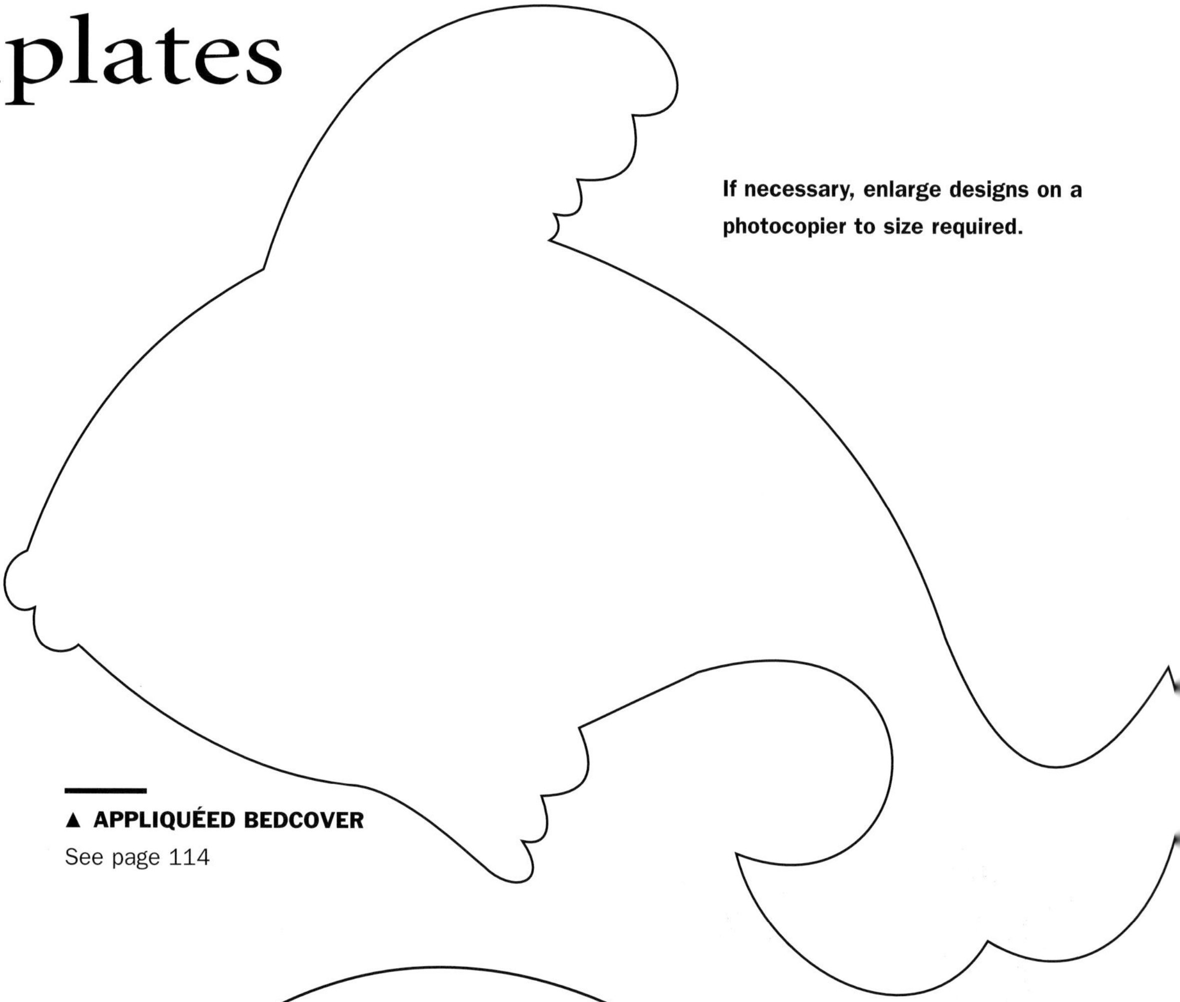

▲ **APPLIQUÉED BEDCOVER**
See page 114

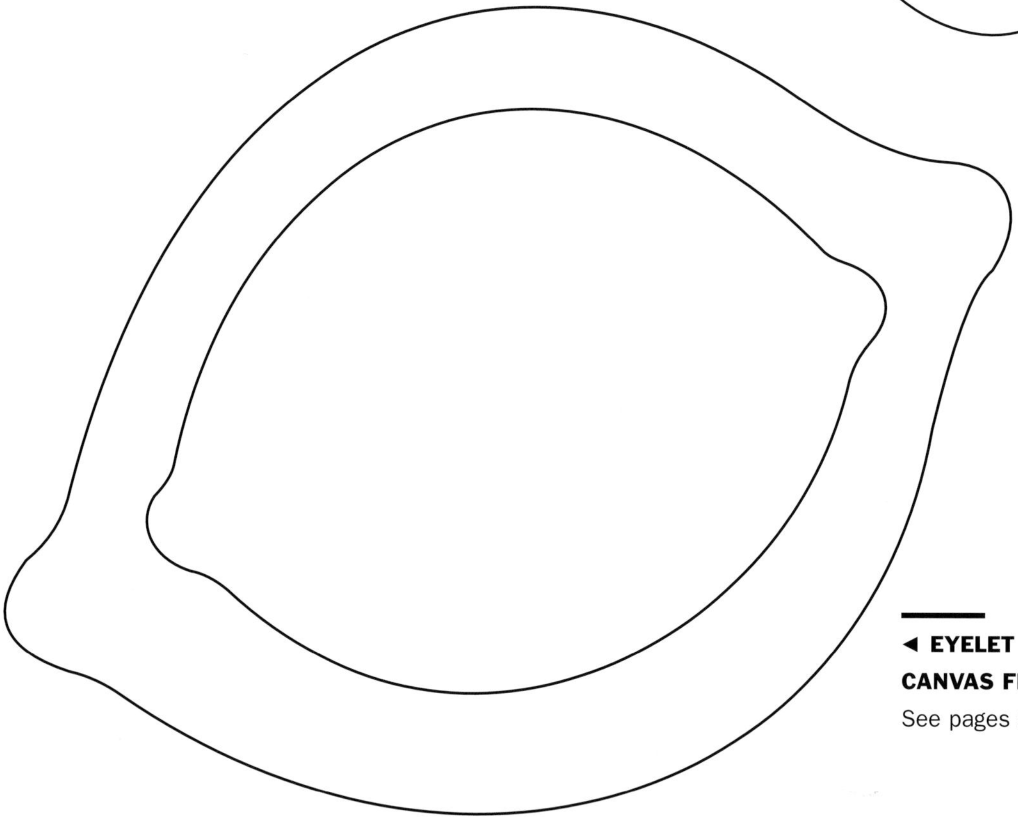

◄ **EYELET BLIND, PELMET,
CANVAS FLOOR MAT**
See pages 50, 52, 59

TEMPLATES

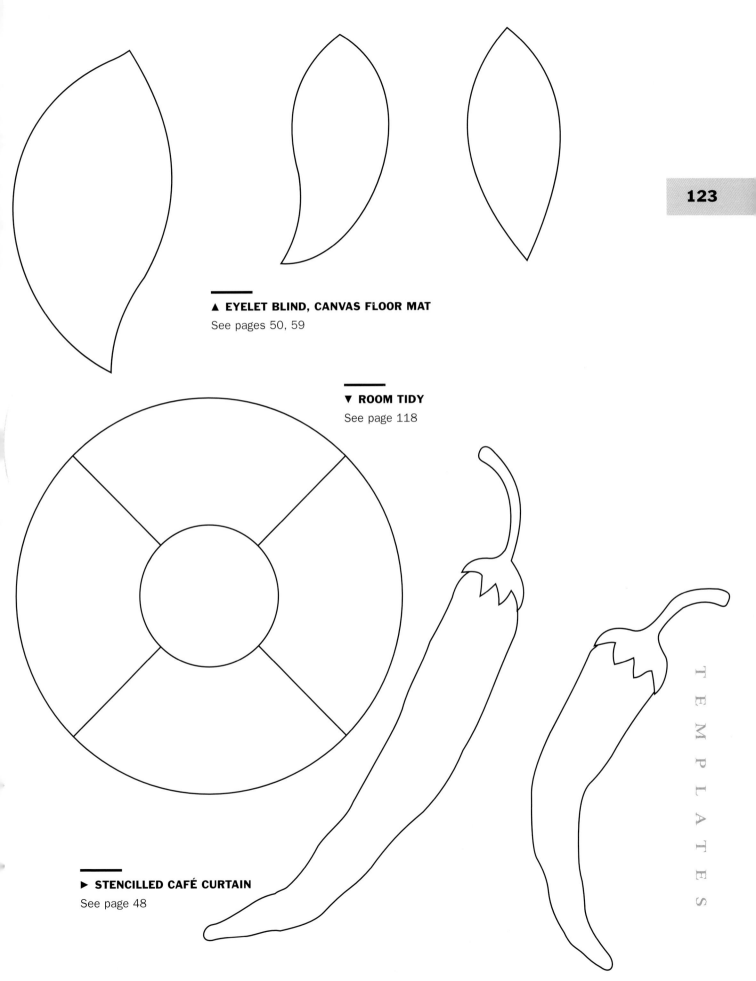

▲ **EYELET BLIND, CANVAS FLOOR MAT**
See pages 50, 59

▼ **ROOM TIDY**
See page 118

► **STENCILLED CAFÉ CURTAIN**
See page 48

TEMPLATES

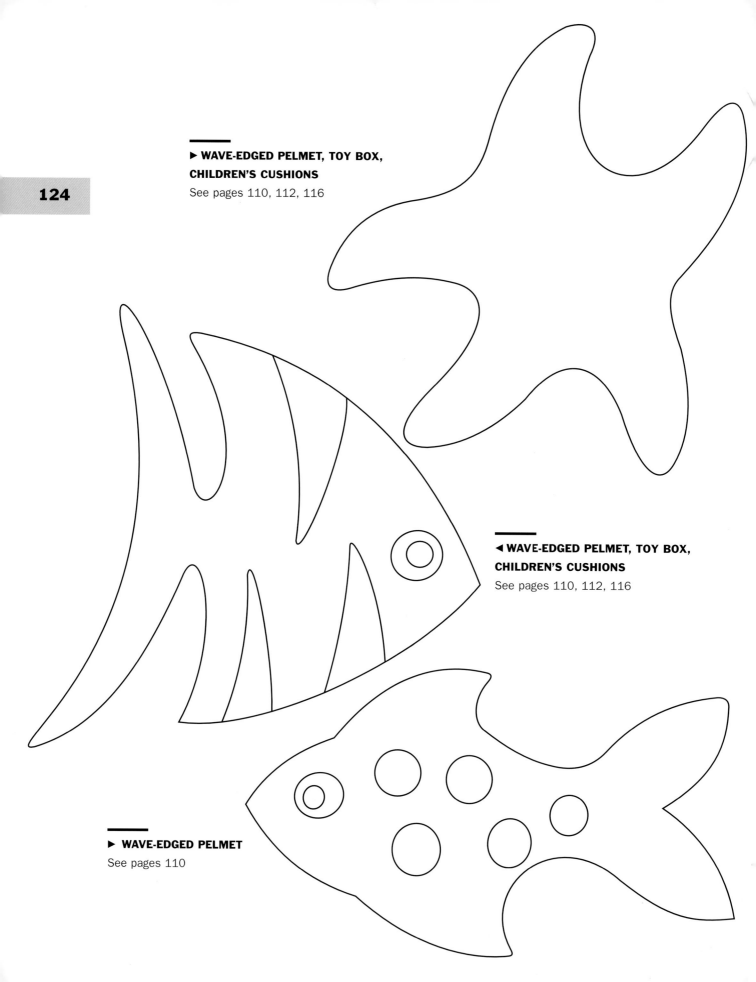

▶ **WAVE-EDGED PELMET, TOY BOX,**
CHILDREN'S CUSHIONS

See pages 110, 112, 116

◀ **WAVE-EDGED PELMET, TOY BOX,**
CHILDREN'S CUSHIONS

See pages 110, 112, 116

▶ **WAVE-EDGED PELMET**

See pages 110

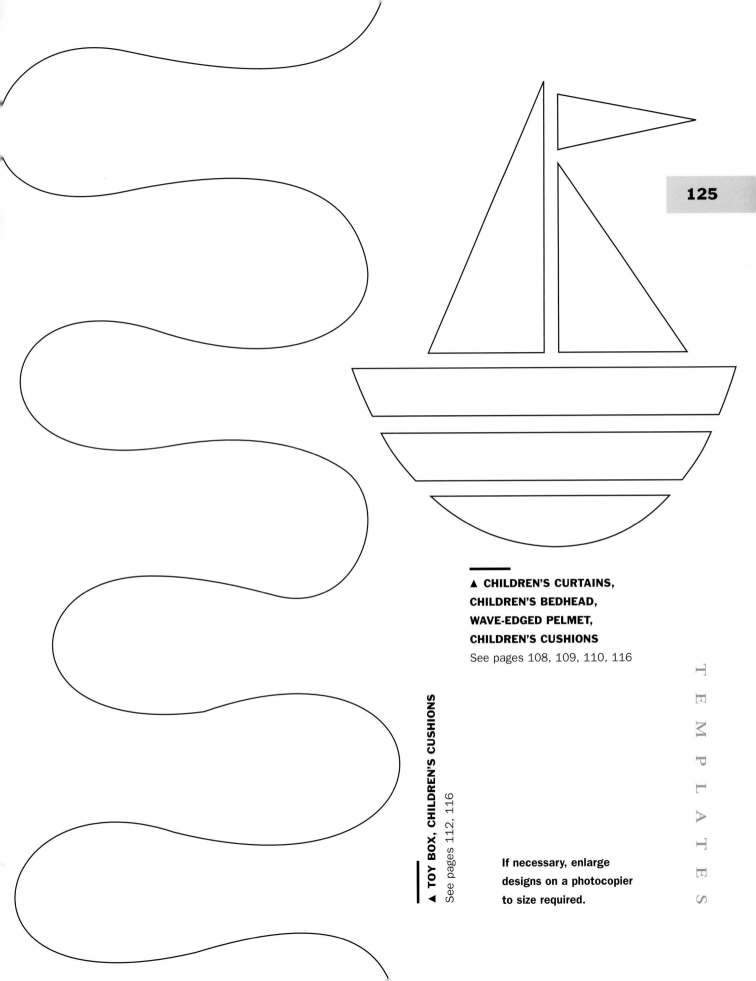

▲ CHILDREN'S CURTAINS,
CHILDREN'S BEDHEAD,
WAVE-EDGED PELMET,
CHILDREN'S CUSHIONS
See pages 108, 109, 110, 116

▲ TOY BOX, CHILDREN'S CUSHIONS
See pages 112, 116

If necessary, enlarge
designs on a photocopier
to size required.

T E M P L A T E S

If necessary, enlarge designs on a
photocopier to size required.

▲ CHILDREN'S CURTAINS
See page 108

▲ CHILDREN'S CUSHIONS
See page 116

Stockists

U.K.
Bostik Ltd
Ulverscraft Road
Leicester LE4 6BW
tel: 0116 251 0015
glue guns and glue sticks

Cover Up Designs Ltd
9 Kingsclere Park
Kingsclere
Nr Newbury
Berks RG20 4SW
tel: 01635 297981/2/3
trimming used on the loose
cover for the sofa

Dylon International
Worsley Bridge Road
Lower Sydenham
London SE26 5HD
tel: 0181 663 4801
fabric dyes for tablecloth,
napkins and four poster
tieback

French Fabric Direct and
Fin-des-siècles
41 Blackford Road
Edinburgh EH92DT
tel: 0131 667 8125
French provençal fabrics for
squab cushion, tablecloth,
napkins and toile de Jouy
on four poster bed

Offray Ribbons
Fir Tree Place
Church Road
Ashford
Middlesex TW15 2AP
tel: 01784 247281
ribbons used throughout
the book

Rufflette Ltd
Sharston Road
Manchester M22 4TH
tel: 0161 998 1811
trims, café clips, no-sew
header tape for curtains,
Pelmform for pelmets

Selectus Ltd
The Uplands
Biddulph
Stoke-on-Trent SG8 7RH
tel: 01782 522316
Velcro

Speedy Products
Speedy House
Cheltenham Street
Salford M6 6WY
tel: 0161 737 1001
no-sew lampshade kit,
no-sew tiebacks

Vilene Retail
P.O. Box 3
Greetland
Halifax HX4 8NJ
tel: 01422 313131
Bondaweb, Funtex,
Bondahem, Wundaweb

Whitehead Fabrics Ltd
14 Hazelwood Close
Hazelwood Trading Estate
Worthing
West Sussex BN14 8NP
tel: 01903 212222
fabrics in the home office

U.S.A.
Ashbrook & Associates
1271N Blue Gum
Anaheim
CA 92806
tel: 714 666 8235
Rufflette products

C M Offray & Son Inc
Route 24
Box 601
Chester
NJ 07930/0601
tel: 908 879 4700
ribbons

Freudenberg Nonwovens-
Northeast
1040 Avenue of the
Americas
New York
NY 10018
tel: 212 391 9020
Vilene products

Handler Textile
Corporation
24 Empire Boulevard
Moonachie
NJ 07074
tel: 201 641 4500
fusible webbing, no-sew
lampshade facings

Prym-dritz Corporation
P. O. Box 5028
Spartanburg
SC 29304
tel: 864 576 5050
Dylon dyes

S-B Power Tool
Corporation
4300 West Peterson
Peterson
Chicago
IL 60646
tel: 312 286 7330
glue guns

Velcro Corporation
406 Brown Avenue
Manchester
NH 03108
tel: 603 669 4880

AUSTRALIA
Bentron
1 Queen street
Auburn
NSW 2144
tel: 02 646 2335
Offray ribbons

Freudenberg Pty. Ltd
P. O. Box 259
3 Brand Drive
Thomastown
VIC 3074
tel: 03 9464 1022
Vilene products

E C Birch
153 Bridge Road
Richmond
Melbourne
VIC 3121
tel: 03 429 4944
fusible webbing, no-sew
lampshade facings

Jackel Pty. Ltd
Jackel House
32 South Street
Rydalmere
NSW 2116
tel: 02 9684 2533
Dylon dyes

Robert Bosch (Australia)
Pty. Ltd
P O Box 66
Rosebank
Clayton
VIC 3169
tel: 03 541 5555
glue guns

Velcro Corporation
Australia
5-11 David Lee Road
Hallam
VIC 3803
tel: 03 9703 2466

Index

ACKNOWLEDGEMENTS
The author and the publishers would like to thank the following people who were so generous with their materials:

Bostik Ltd; Cover Up Designs Ltd; Dylon International Ltd; French Fabric Direct; Offray Ribbons; Rufflette Ltd; Speedy Products; Vilene Retail; Whitehead Fabrics Ltd.

Although the name on a book cover is that of the author, making books such as these is always team work. So I would like to thank everyone who worked so hard to put this book together. This includes Alma Caira, Rosemary Wilkinson and Shona Wood, as well as my au pair, Sophie Ankarswed, who kept us sane with tea, coffee and delicious lunches.